The Skier's Handbook

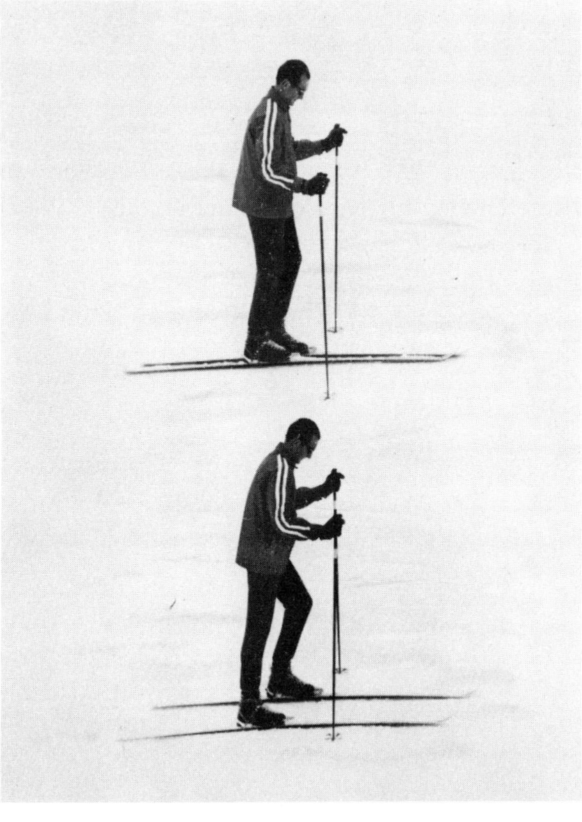

Traverse Sidestep

This movement allows the skier to traverse the hill while climbing. It is a combination of the sidestep with the walking exercise. There is a complete weight transfer to the upper ski in an unbroken motion.

Herringbone

Start with both skis firmly planted in the snow. The weight transfer frees one ski for the step up the slope. The pole opposite the ski being lifted supports the skier.

Kick Turn

The kick turn is a complete change of direction from a standstill. One ski is kicked up and swung around to face the tail of the other ski. Then, in one motion, the other ski and pole are brought around next to the moved ski and pole.

Straight Running

Together with the snowplow, straight running is one of the two final forms of Class A, the first or novice class of the American system. The skier who feels confident of trying a shallow slope should remember that it is not only a question of form but also a question of flexibility. The American system final forms are not rigid molds to be copied by all skiers; they merely demonstrate certain basics. Attempt the form in a relaxed manner. It is more important that the skier shift and keep balanced on uneven terrain than that he look exactly like the final form at every second of his descent.

Straight running is the direct descent of the slope. Feet are together, skis are flat on the snow equally weighted and body is at a right angle to the slope. Knees, ankles and hips are flexed so that the legs can absorb the shock of terrain changes without upsetting the equilibrium of the body. Equal pressure should be maintained on the balls and heels of the feet. Balance is achieved by flexing the legs only, the upper body always remaining erect. Hands and poles are carried in a relaxed manner, baskets to the rear. Except for the degree of bending in the legs, the degree of slope does not affect the stance.

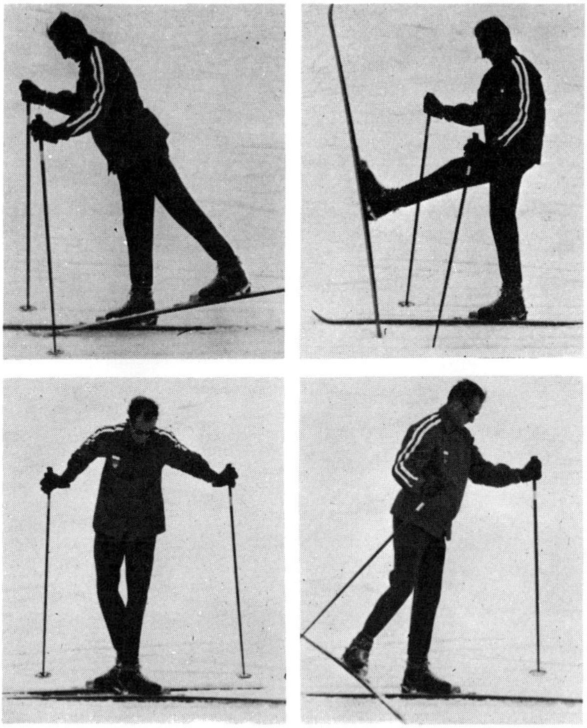

The Snowplow

This is the first means of control that most skiers learn. It should be emphasized, however, that the dangers of the snowplow are not so much in the maneuver itself as in the secure feeling of the position, with the result that some skiers feel it necessary to descend an entire slope in the snowplow. This is seldom necessary. Moreover it can lead to the problem of "snowplow fixation." This means the skier never goes on to the more flexible if slightly more demanding method of alternating straight running with the snowplow. The skier should practice shifting from one form to the other form while underway down the slope.

To do the snowplow, simply push out the tails of your skis, keeping the tips together. This should be done with a gentle brushing motion. Avoid jerkiness, keep your knees well flexed and hold your body erect. Except for angling the skis inward, the snowplow stance is essentially the same as for straight running. The skis will ride slightly on their inside edges, the knees being closer together than the feet, and this, combined with the V angle of the skis, produces the plow effect. Be careful not to overdo the edging by pressing the knees together as this will lock you into a cramped position. To increase the braking power, simply push the tails out farther and flex more in the knees and ankles. The snowplow should not be used as a means of stopping suddenly; it is used to control your speed on a gentle slope. Do not expect immediate results, for it may be some yards before you notice much slowing. So, anticipate the need to slow down, brush out the ski tails, stay relaxed and wait for the plow to act. As in straight running, try to maintain equal pressure on the balls and heels of your feet. Also, make sure that each leg is equally flexed and that your body is kept between the skis.

SKI POINTERS FOR THE NOVICE CLASS

Save Strength in Climbing

by Marcel Barel, Certified, FWSIA

It's smart to save your strength when you ski, whether you are just out for a few runs or whether you plan to be skiing for a week. Since climbing is involved in almost all skiing, the easier and more relaxed you make your climbing the more you'll have left for the downhill run.

Most skiers are tempted to sidestep when faced with a climb. It's easy and direct. *However, the long way round, a series of easy zig-zags up the hill, will get you there nearly as fast and in much better shape.*

If you think about it, you can develop an eye for terrain. In the illustration, the climber is taking the easy route to get to the same point that a preceding skier sidestepped in a more tiring route. The climber has angled up to a relatively level spot where he will make a kick or a step turn and then proceed (solid line) up to the top. His eye picked out the level spot and selected the route before he began to climb. This knack, indispensable in any kind of touring, is useful in all skiing.

Go Backward to Progress

by John Bailey, Certified, SRMSIA

Beginning skiers need three things: confidence, fun and the feel of correct body position—in whatever order you like. A backward-moving snowplow turn from a herringbone position is one exercise that supplies the sense of all three accomplishments and does it in a single exercise. It automatically teaches correct ankle bend, control of edging with the knees, control of speed by edging and correct weight shift using the upper body only. All of these things happen when you try to do the backward plow. To perform the exercise, take the herringbone climbing position, let the skis "flatten" against the snow until you start moving backward down the hill. You will find that edging the skis again (by turning them on edge with knee pressure) will make you stop. By putting most of your weight on one ski, while moving backward, you will turn in one direction or the other. After experimenting with the backward-plow turn, left and right, you will find you are ready to employ the mechanics of a normal snowplow, going frontward down the hill with the tips together and keeping the tails of the skis out. You have gone backward to progress forward.

Two Pole Turnaround

by O. L. Smith, Certified, CUSSA

Before a skier can learn to ski downhill, he has to learn to turn and face downhill, using his poles in some way to hold himself stationary until he's headed in the right direction. There are a lot of wrong ways of doing this. The right way is to put the two poles downhill of his tips and then walk the skis into position. Here is the secret of doing this easily. *Put the butt end of the pole handle in the palm of each hand and then extend both poles downhill, about two feet apart, until the elbows are straight. Plant the poles in the snow (elbows still straight) so that you can lean forward slightly on the poles, making sure that you have a straight line now between the basket of the pole and your shoulder. Maintain this position as you step the tails of the skis uphill.* There will be very little strain on your muscles, because, in this technique, the bones of the arm take all the weight. You will find you can step your skis around easily and go right into that gravity-powered run simply by bending your elbows and thus letting the skis start forward. But until you want to start down, keep the elbows straight.

Doing the Kick Turn Easily

by Bill Briggs, Certified, FWSIA

Here is a way of keeping in perfect balance during the execution of a kick turn. First, place both poles in the snow four to five feet uphill of the skis, three to four feet apart. Now put the handles of the poles in the small of your back, hands well up on the poles so the gloves cushion the poles against your back. Then lean against the poles solidly. If the poles are placed correctly, you should be leaning just very slightly out of the vertical at this point. Now raise the tip of the downhill ski very smoothly. *The trick here is not to turn your body at all until you have planted the tail of the ski in the snow.* Once you have planted the ski and held it a second, let the tip swing easily and smoothly to the tail of your other ski. Then you can recover your vertical stance simply by bending forward at the waist until you are balanced over the downhill ski. The uphill ski can then be picked up and placed parallel to the downhill one.

Quick Kick Turn

by Ken Barnes, Certified, NRMSIA, RMSIA

The kick turn is probably the most useful thing a beginning skier can master. When he gets it, he can save himself a lot of walking around corners and a lot of backing down from the edge of the slope.

The key to a quick and easy kick turn: swing the downhill ski straight up and set the tail of the ski into the snow gently. From there, let it fall easily into the snow, pointing the opposite direction of the uphill ski.

The great problem is the fact that skiers often tense leg muscles during the kick turn. This makes it impossible to complete the turn easily. So, in order to relax, make sure of your balance by doing this:

Kick the ski up to the vertical position, then bring it back to the starting position. If you can do this well in balance, then you will have no trouble with the turn.

If you find the exercise uncomfortable, then check the position of your poles (wide enough apart?) and the point at which you rested the tail (close to the first ski is correct). Try it again, several times, until you find you can do it easily. Then do the kick turn from start to finish.

Stand Upright

by Frank Day, Certified, USEASA

Although seemingly elementary, the simple fact of proper basic stance is often overlooked as being unimportant. It is not. In spite of the fact that most people think the basic posture involves a bend forward at the waist, this is not so. Unless you need a forward bend from the waist to get your weight ahead for a given maneuver, then good posture on skis is the same as good posture when walking: upright. *You should have a slight bend in the knees, and a corresponding bend in the hip joint (not the waist) so that the two large masses of weight (chest and hips) are lined up, one directly over the other.* In this way, your weight is supported by your skeletal bones, particularly by a straight spinal column. The pelvis is vertical as well. In the incorrect position pictured on opposite page, right, the forward bend at the waist causes your back muscles to be strained while you ski. Your pelvis tips forward, causing a strain, as well, on the upper thigh muscles. You will tire quite quickly. Therefore, get used to the restful upright position and stick with it. The incorrect stance tends to straighten the legs so that you lose the loose flexibility you should have in order to compensate for the rise and fall of the terrain.

Rocking to Relax

by Richard Corey, Certified, CUSSA

A good, relaxed body position is almost impossible to maintain if your feet hurt. And so, it's a good idea to make sure the feet are relaxed once or twice during your ski day, particularly during the afternoon.

A relaxed foot is a foot that is flat in the boot. If it starts to tense, the foot quickly starts to hurt. *To keep your foot relaxed and flat, try this. First, take a normal stance on the flat. Then lean forward so that the pressure under the heel in your boot diminishes. Then rock back (see illustration) so that the tip of your toe touches the inside top of the boot. Now go forward again until your weight is on the ball of the foot. Repeat this rocking a couple of times, and it will relax the feet.* It will also leave the leg muscles feeling more relaxed. Now, when you start to ski, keep the foot flat and just keep the weight forward to the point where the ankle puts a bit of pressure against the tongue of the boot. This is where you should be skiing.

Pre-run Check List

by Chuck Quinn, Certified, ISIA; Member, PSIA

It seems that proper position plays an important part in the success of anything we do. Good body position is especially important in skiing. It is an absolute necessity in skiing deep powder and difficult snow, such as we find in the spring.

I have always felt that if you start in the correct position you have a better chance of maintaining it throughout your run. So before beginning a run, get into position by going over this check list: (*1*) *Are your ankles pressed together and forward to the maximum? This gets you "locked in" and helps you to stay evenly weighted.* (*2*) *Are your knees pressed together and forward toward the tips of your skis? This again gives you that "locked in" feeling, preventing the snow from forcing your skis apart. And it gets you down low.* (*3*) *Is your chin tucked in? pulling your chin in straightens your back and prevents you from bending forward from the waist, which, of course, causes the tips to dive.*

Use this check list before each run: ankles, knees and chin. And if you come all apart—stop and start again. Remember, always start a run in position.

Getting Up

by Louis Gheller, Certified, CUSSA

If you find yourself in an awkward position after a spill, and you cannot get your skis properly under you for the standard getting-up procedure, try the following: *hook the basket of your downhill pole over the tip of the downhill ski. Grip the pole with the thumb of the hand pointing toward the basket. Put the knuckles of your uphill hand into the snow next to your uphill hip. Push against the snow with your knuckles, and pull with the hand that holds the ski pole. You will rise easily off the snow.*

Be sure to set your edges as you rise. Otherwise you will find yourself sideslipping in a very unnatural position for sideslipping.

This method is especially good for icy conditions. It helps get weight forward, and it keeps the skis from slipping away as you rise.

Heave-ho Get Up

by Janet Wagner, Certified, CSIA

Even after learning the standard technique for getting up, skiers still have trouble making that last couple of inches needed to get upright. So, here follows a way of helping you to overcome gravity by bringing the big leg muscles into play: first, arrange the body with skis downhill and pointed level across the slope. Second, pull the knees up to the chest. Third, put the pole tips in the snow next to the hip, so you can put one hand over the pole baskets and the other over the pole handles. Now, *rock back a bit and then forcefully throw the upper body forward toward the ski tips.* Do this in rhythmic stages: Heave! (lean back), Ho! (forward) and Hup! (get up). The last step requires a normal amount of push from the lower hand and pull from the upper hand. Then the movement of the upper body gives the legs room to work and up you come!

Raising Your Status

by Penny Brown

Some fairly strong skiers find no trouble at all in getting up from a fall with the use of the poles: they stick the poles in the snow and lever themselves upright.

For the majority, however, there is a somewhat easier way.

Once you are down, get squared away so that the feet are straight down the hill from your body and the legs extended so that they are practically straight.

Put your poles down.

Next, put the uphill hand on the snow and lift your hips off the snow (see illustration). Then move the underneath ski up under the hips, placing the ski as flat on the snow and as close to your hand as you can. Now inch your hand down to your ski. At this point your weight is pretty much over your uphill ski and you can squat over it without any trouble.

Bring your other ski under you and you can stand up on both skis.

Replacing Skis After a Fall

by Norm Bergerson, Certified, CUSSA

After a fall when your ski has come off, it is sometimes difficult to get the ski back on. It may be that you are on a steep slope, or that the snow is boiler-plate hard. In either case, it is easier to put on an uphill ski than a downhill ski, so, if it is possible, turn yourself so the foot that lost the ski is uphill. Then start putting on the ski. From this position if the ski should start to slide sideways, you can stop it. Jam your poles in the snow to act as an obstacle. *Once you are in position to replace the ski, take your mittens and put them on the snow under your loose ski.* Then the ski will stay in one place while you are scraping the snow off your boot sole (this should always be done) and putting the boot back into the binding. It's always a good idea to stamp the newly refastened ski on the snow a couple of times to make sure your heel and toe fastenings are well-seated on the boot. Then press the leg forward; this is a final test of the security of the binding. Lastly, don't tear off in a hurry as if to make up for lost time. The fall may have been a warning you are getting tired. Make one or two nice rounded school turns in perfect control before you decide to open up again.

Replacing Skis in Deep Snow

by Calvin Beisswanger, Certified, CUSSA; Member, PSIA

Some snow conditions (deep powder, wet stuff) make it difficult to put your boot back into the binding in the middle of the run. About the best way to get a boot back into the binding free of snow and seated firmly is to stick the tail of the ski well down into the snow while you put the boot back in.

There are two or three small tricks to make this work well.

First, make a platform for the ski still bound by stamping it into the snow so you can stand without slipping.

Second, push the loose ski as far into the snow as it can go while still leaving the binding out.

Third, a steep angle is more likely to work for you than a shallow angle. Stick the ski into the snow around thirty to forty-five degrees from vertical. (See illustration.)

This way, once you have the boot and binding clean, you can put the boot back in the binding without getting a pad of snow between you and the ski.

Rise and Plow

by John Kronsnoble, Certified, CUSSA; Member, PSIA

When a skier is trying to execute the snowplow as a braking mechanism, his position may be too rigid to have the edge control necessary to flatten the skis. This means the tails of the skis cannot be brushed out easily into the snowplow position.

A skier who has any trouble at all getting into the plow position ought to try the following. While still running down the slope with skis together, do a deep knee bend. Do it once, slowly. Then do it a second time, coming up quickly. *As you come up, push the tails of the skis apart. You will find that they brush into the plow position quite easily.*

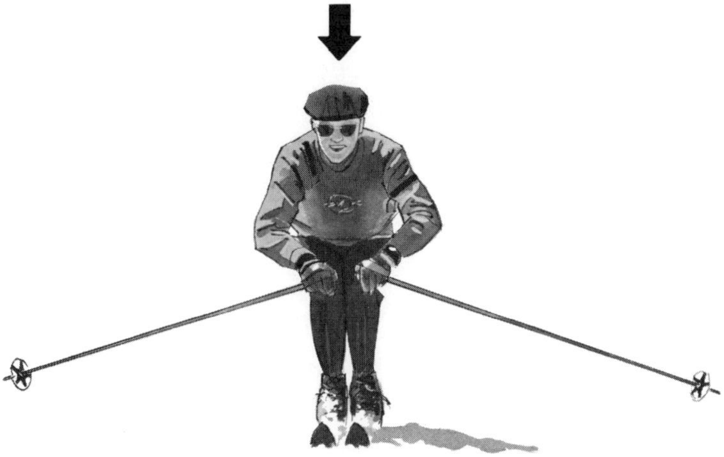

Scotch the Stingy Plow

by Murdo MacDonald, Certified, USEASA

Beginners find that the wider their snowplow, the more the tips of their skis will cross. So they soon tend to keep the tails of their skis no more than two to three feet apart, or less. But this "stingy plow" will not control your speed in a turn. The narrow stance limits the movement of the upper body by which you shift the weight onto the outside ski to make your turns. This means you cannot get enought weight onto the outside ski. The turn is weak; it swings wide and fast instead of short and controlled. The weak swing keeps you in the fall line longer and you accelerate. *So it is better to force the tails of the skis three to four feet apart.* Control the tips by pushing apart from the hips and not from the knees. A knock-kneed position lets the tips cross. With a wide plow you now shift weight effectively and make nice, short, controlled turns.

III. *Beginner Class*

In this section we deal with the snowplow turn and the traverse. The snowplow turn is a devoutly-to-be-wished-for consummation of the first day on skis, because it means that not only downhill speed but downhill direction can be controlled by the skier, enabling him to negotiate trails and slopes rather than shooting down them in an uncontrolled fashion.

Snowplow Turn

The snowplow turn is a matter of putting more weight on one ski than on the other. The weighted ski will steer more than the lightened ski and so both skis will turn. In the straight snowplow you have been trying to keep equal weight on each ski. In the snowplow turn, you will put as much of your weight as you can on the ski that is going to steer you around. The weighting of the ski is facilitated by bringing back somewhat the shoulder nearest that ski. This is called the "counter." The shoulder counters and the knee over the weighted ski is bent with a sinking motion of the body. Don't try to twist the ski around, let the weight do the work. Skis stay at the same angle through the turn. Put plenty of weight on the steering ski; don't edge the steering ski too much; look down the hill, not up the hill; make sure you counter the shoulder and angle the body over the weighted ski.

Weight Shift for the Snowplow Turn

The shift of the weight to the outside of the turn is one of the factors that starts the skis turning. Emphasis on a decisive, smooth weight shift is a key principle in the American system. The skier starts going straight down the hill and shifts his weight to the outside ski to begin the turn. To keep the turn underway, the skier maintains steady weighting of the outside ski of the turn. If he doesn't shift his weight, he continues downhill without turning.

The Traverse

This final form is often learned in conjunction with the snowplow turn. It is a path across the hill, or across the "fall line," a term which simply refers to a line following the steepest part of the hill. The traverse can be at right angles to the fall line (this is a "dead traverse"), but most of the time it is slanted somewhat more down the hill so that the skier gets a bit of speed as he traverses.

A traverse in which the skier accelerates rapidly is called a steep traverse, and at this point the word "traverse" rapidly loses its usefulness, because it becomes indistinguishable from straight running, with approximately the same results.

Note that skis in the process of turning are not technically traversing. The traverse comes at the end of the turn and before the next turn, when the skis are running straight.

To traverse properly: the uphill ski, hip and shoulder are slightly advanced, skis are close together, more weight on lower ski, upper body is angled over the weighted ski.

SKI POINTERS FOR THE BEGINNER CLASS

Lean Out

by Hans Jenni, Certified, USEASA

Most falls occur toward the hill rather than down the hill. The reason that most falls occur into the hill is that the skier is not standing correctly on his skis. Most skiers seem to be afraid they will fall down the slope, so they lean in toward the hill, particularly when they are traversing.

What happens then is that the weight goes on the uphill ski, and it will tend to slide down the hill and strike the downhill ski so that the skier's support is knocked clean out from under him.

If, on the other hand, you will practice leaning out from the slope (see illustration), then the weight stays off the uphill ski and stays on the downhill ski where it belongs. *You will find that you will stand up as long as you lean—out.*

The Pointable Navel

by Jim and Joy Lucas, Certified, PSNIA

Beginning skiers who are learning to traverse often have trouble because the uphill ski "splits" and heads uphill, away from the other ski. This makes it probable that the beginner will fall backward into the hill. To prevent this, the trick is to make sure that practically all the weight is kept on the downhill ski. A sure way to accomplish this trick is to think of this phrase, *"point the belly button down the hill."* With the "button" pointed down the hill, the uphill shoulder and ski are automatically advanced. If the lower leg is now bent, the skier's weight goes on it (see illustration). As a result, you will attain the proper traverse position as it is defined in the American system of skiing. The skis stay together across the hill. The weight stays on the downhill ski. You stay over the skis. You are easily able to perform the basic traverse maneuver that gets you across the hill to the place where you are going to start your next turn.

Baskets Up the Hill

by Miner Patton, Certified, PNSIA

Often a beginning skier will find that he slips downhill when traversing across a steep slope. But steepness is just a mental block, and can be combatted by use of the right technique. The steeper the slope which you are traversing, the more weight you must apply on the downhill ski. To really get the weight down on the lower ski, your body must face somewhat downhill. The simplest way for a beginning skier to remember how his body should be oriented at *all* times, except when actually in a turn or going straight down the hill, is to say to himself "Baskets up the hill." *If the baskets of the poles are up the hill, then hands, shoulders and hips normally assume the proper relationship to the skis.* (See illustration.) That is, hands are turned downhill, and the upper body is facing somewhat downhill. Add the words, "Weight on the downhill ski," and the formula is complete. If you remember to say to yourself, "Baskets up the hill," you won't skid sideways down steep sections you must cross in order to reach the easier terrain.

Getting the Right Angle

by Max Dercum, Certified, RMSIA; Member, PSIA

The proper position of the entire body during a traverse of a steeper slope is the same as the proper position on an average slope, with the exception of increased comma. This means that on the steeper, as on the average slope, the lines through the shoulders, hips and across the toes of the boots are all parallel, with the downhill shoulder, hip and boot slightly back. (See illustrations.)

If the skier meets trouble on a traverse across a steep slope, it is because he forgets to increase his comma or angulation. You will note how the increased angle of upper and lower body in the illustration (opposite page, right) puts more weight on the downhill ski and helps hold firm on a steep hill where a lesser angle, such as in the illustration (opposite page, left) would not hold.

The steeper the hill, the greater the angle of the comma.

How to Come Across

by Tom Barrett, Certified, USEASA

To become proficient in the American Ski Technique as it is being taught in many areas throughout the country today, it is necessary to have full confidence in your ability to perform one basic position: the traverse. This is the position you must maintain between turns. As you finish one turn and move across the hill toward your next turn, you will be traversing. Many mistakes in skiing start with a badly executed traverse. Here is how to do a good one. Place your skis across the hill in such a position that they can't slide either forward or backward. Advance your uphill ski ahead about one half a boot length and put your weight over the downhill ski. *Allow your body to relax in this position and look toward the far side of the trail* toward the spot where your next turn will start. (If you are a golfer, think of it this way: you are about thirty yards off the green and are positioning yourself for an easy chip shot.) Your knees are flexed and your hips and shoulders are turned somewhat downhill. Move up and down slightly, using knee, ankle and hip joints as you go across the hill. This relaxed traverse position will enable you to start your next turn quickly and at the spot where you want to start it.

Double Check the Angles

by Dick Johnson, Certified, FWSIA

Nearly all skiers have a certain amount of trouble maintaining a steadfast traverse when conditions get a bit icy or when the hill falls away steeply: either the lower ski slips down or the tails of both skis slip down. A good deal of this trouble is derived from improper body position. Double check your body position as soon as you begin to move. The weight is on the downhill ski. The uphill ski is advanced so that a line between the ski tips will strike an angle to your path (see illustration). This is the same angle which should be present in similar imaginary lines (see illustration) drawn through the toes, knees, hips, hands and shoulders. *You will find that by double checking all these angles you will improve your comma position and thereby give yourself a smooth steady traverse,* capable of holding on any kind of boiler-plate or on the steepest of pitches. One added point: the steeper or icier the slope, the more emphatic the outward lean of the comma. Greater lean puts greater pressure on the lower ski, and it is the lower ski that does the holding for you.

Bounce to Better Skiing

by Rhona Gillis, Certified, CSIA

This is more of a mind-improver than a style-improver: however, remember you ski with your confidence as well as your skis. If you have a moment of feeling that the prospect of going down the next fifty feet is dreary and not inviting, generate the feeling of all-will-be-great by doing a little traverse from the point where you are standing to another point across the hill, and *bounce* as you go across.

Often you will find that the moment the muscles feel free and limber, the mind feels the same, and you will go down the slope wondering what it was that you were worrying about.

The effect of bouncing not only warms the heart but it actually unfreezes the reactions that you need to make even one turn on the bunny slope.

The antidote for dead-on-the-skis is ten or fifteen bounces, taken immediately.

Uphill Ski Ahead

by Hans Jenni, Certified, USEASA

If you have ever taken a ski lesson at the beginner level, you have heard the ski instructor say "Uphill ski ahead." There's a good reason for this. Whenever you are traversing across a hill, the tip of the uphill ski will tend to slip down across the downhill ski—*unless* you keep the uphill ski ahead. This "uphill ski ahead" position makes it impossible for the uphill ski to cross the downhill ski. If the uphill ski starts to cross, then the uphill tip just comes to rest against the tip of the downhill ski and no harm is done.

Should you forget this simple precaution, just put all your weight on the downhill ski and merely lift the uphill ski off the snow, straighten it out and put it where it belongs: uphill and ahead.

If you find you are constantly forgetting to keep the uphill ski ahead, do this. *Press the downhill leg against the uphill leg so that the downhill knee fits into the bend back of the uphill knee. Traverse a smooth slope with legs locked in this position for a while and you'll soon get the feel of having the uphill ski ahead.*

IV. *Intermediate Class*

Now the skier is ready for more sophisticated maneuvers. The stem turn, sideslipping and the uphill christie will concern us here. The basic form of each is to be learned in order that the logical progression to the more advanced movements of the American Technique may be made.

The Stem Turn

This first final form of the American system Class C marks a milestone in the skier's progress. It combines the snowplow turn with the traverse, allowing for travel across the trail in a much more rapid manner than with the snowplow turn alone. In the snowplow turn, the skier is always braking. In the stem turn, he stops braking as he comes into the traverse position and glides easily across the slope to the point where the next turn begins.

To make a stem turn, brush out the tail of the uphill ski, pulling the tip slightly back at the same time. Up to this point, the weight should be carried on the lower ski. Now pull back the uphill shoulder a little and press it down toward the foot as you would for a snowplow turn. The weight will now be over the stemmed ski and, of its own accord, it will turn into and through the fall line. Once again, do not try to force the turn; just wait for it to happen. At the end of the turn, your outside ski will be the lower ski of a new traverse. Your weight will already be over it in the correct manner and all you need to do is straighten up a little and pull in the unweighted tail of the new uphill ski. You will notice that your shoulders, hips and uphill lead ski will already be in the correct positions for the new traverse as a result of your preparations for the turn.

Counter Rotation

Counter rotation is the movement of the upper body in the direction opposite the turn. In the American system, beginning skiers in the stem turn are taught to make a slight counter motion (top, opposite page) so they will be familiar with it by the time they come to advanced turns. It is also recognized that moving the shoulders exactly opposite to the skis greatly improves balance. The skier (below, opposite page) making the turn without counter rotation will have to learn the movement later, anyway.

Angulation

At the same time that a skier makes the counter movement, he also leans his upper body over the outside ski of the turn (above, opposite page). This makes it easier to put weight on that ski and to turn the ski up on edge, both of which are necessary to turn. Failure to angulate (below, opposite page) makes it hard to weight the outside ski and edge it, so the resulting turn is slow and unsure. The American system stresses edge control by body angulation rather than by ankle or knee alone.

Sideslip

The sideslip is the second final form in Class C. It is the transition from a steered or stemmed turn to the fine feeling of a sliding or slipped turn. (The sliding turn is referred to in skiing as the "christie" turn.) Learning the sideslip is to unlearn the hard bite of the edging that the good traverse position requires. Sideslip edging is relaxed. The ski must slip sideways down the hill. Sideslipping is also a useful maneuver, since it often affords the easiest descent over a given spot. The skier who spends some time getting his ankle muscles accustomed to the feeling of letting go has made the best possible investment in his future on skis.

Forward Sideslip

From a traverse, the sideslip is started with a slight up-weighting, the angulation is eliminated and this flattens the skis, resulting in a sideslip.

Sideslip with Poles

This exercise is designed to provide transition from the forward sideslip to the vertical sideslip. Poles are placed in the snow uphill of the skier; the skier then uses the poles to push the skis downhill.

Vertical Sideslip

The vertical sideslip is started with a slight up motion from a standing traverse position.

Uphill Christie

The last of the Class C forms is the very first taste of "christie skiing." In its simplest form, the uphill christie is a traverse, followed by a sideslip, followed by a turning of the ski tails downhill. Start with a traverse, rise to make a sideslip, then sink again, thrust the heels downward and outward. Power rather than speed is what you need. Just push slowly but purposefully, holding your chest well toward the valley and pushing down on your heels with a slight grinding action, as though you were grinding a pair of cigarette butts into the ground. Be careful, however, not to let the hips move outward from the hill. Although they will rotate slightly in the direction of the turn, the hips, together with the knees, must always be held farther into the hill than the upper body. Otherwise, your weight will go onto the uphill ski and your control will be lost immediately.

Unweighting by Up Motion

The skier (above, opposite page) first sinks into a bent-knee position, then pushes upward, carrying his weight off the skis. The unweighted skis can then be swung into the turn. Here up-unweighting is shown as it is used in the uphill christie. This is the first of the sideslipped turns taught in the American system. The figures (below, opposite page) demonstrate how the uphill christie is taught in the Austrian system. It asks the skier to drop his weight suddenly to a lower position and he turns his skis during this drop. The American system uses up-unweighting because it is easier to teach. Up-unweighting keeps the skier's weight off the skis for a longer time than down-unweighting.

SKI POINTERS FOR THE INTERMEDIATE CLASS

Hands at Rest

by Ish Arnold, Certified, USEASA; Member, PSIA

One of the essential things a beginning skier must learn is to keep his balance with a minimum of motion. Too many snowplowing beginners hold their arms in the air like a carrier flagman wig-wagging a plane to a landing. They are, in effect, trying to control themselves with their arms and poles rather than with the legs and skis. Proper ski stance is lost, along with correct control. The poles snag in the snow in front of the skier. The way to avoid the posture problem is to *keep the hands at the midsection* (see illustration). The baskets of the poles will automatically stay back where they belong and where they can be used when you cross level spots. They won't get stuck in front of the skis. It will also keep the body in the correct skiing position. The legs will maintain control of the situation because they won't be fighting the poles.

Double Your Stem

by Paul Brown, Certified, CSIA

Stem christie turns fall into two types: first, the christie initiated by stemming the uphill ski (standard American Technique) and, second, the christie initiated by stemming the downhill ski. The uphill-stem christie makes for easy turns at slower speeds because the uphill ski (which is to become the outside ski of the next turn) is already partly swung in the new direction and is already on its new inside edge. The downhill-stem christie, on the other hand, is more comfortable at higher speeds: it provides a steadying effect prior to the turn and makes a better platform for the unweighting motion. Here is a way to enjoy the advantages of both kinds: *each ski is stemmed an equal amount from the traverse line (see illustration) with the body assuming a comfortable stance square over the skis and centered between them.* Using the "double stem christie" gives you steadying effect and ease of turning, both advantages at once.

Correct Your Cross

by Joe Berry, Certified, USEASA; Member, PSIA

Some beginning skiers find that when they make their first stem turns the tips of their skis start crossing. The cause of the problem may well be that they are not bringing the outside ski of the turn back early enough in the turn. The idea is that with the inside ski tip leading a bit (see illustration), it cannot cross the outside ski. Secondly, since the weight will be mainly on the outside ski, this ski cannot cross the inside ski. Therefore, the best approach is to *bring the uphill ski back as soon as you stem it*. There are added advantages. It is easier to shift the weight to the stemmed outside ski when it is brought back. And, since the outside shoulder is, by rule, brought back at the beginning of the turn, it is a smoother turn if the outside ski is brought back with the shoulder. Just remember to do both things at once and you will find that your tip-cross is corrected and that you can do a series of stem turns more easily.

Sure-fire Sideslip

by Frank Lamphier, Certified, USEASA

The key to a good sideslip is self-evident: both skis have to be almost flat. Unfortunately, most skiers, while they easily flatten the downhill ski, forget to do the same with the uphill ski. Thus, as soon as the sideslip starts, the uphill ski splits away. This throws the skier off balance. To make a good sideslip, first of all, you have to have a good traverse position. Second, you have to flatten both skis (but keep the weight on the downhill ski). A good way to get the uphill ski flat is to *press the uphili knee against the downhill knee (see circle in illustration) thereby flattening both skis together.* Then both your skis are working as one. *Pressing the uphill knee into the downhill one simplifies slipping sideways (see arrow).* It will also make forward sideslipping, stem garlands and parallel garlands easy steps in your progress toward stem christie skiing. Note: good parallel skiers should practice sideslips, as well as intermediates. Many otherwise proficient parallel skiers, when they have occasion to sideslip ten yards or so downhill, forget that a sideslip must be done with the skis flat—both of them.

Hop Slip

by Sepp Walzl, Certified, CSIA

Most skiers want to learn to parallel, and the secret of parallel skiing lies in sideslipping. No one takes enough time to learn sideslipping as thoroughly as he should before going on to try the parallel, or side-slipped, turn.

A good way to work on your sideslip is to traverse normally across a gentle slope, and then come up to lighten the skis (see illustration) and come down gently on flat skis so they will begin to sideslip as well as traverse. This is your forward sideslip, essentially the action of a parallel turn.

You will find that the up motion will start skis sideslipping even in difficult snow conditions. *The better you learn to sideslip the more fun skiing becomes and the sooner you will master parallel skiing.*

Importance of Lean

by Midge Haefeli, Certified, CUSSA

While the skier of average ability will do fairly well in keeping his balance in constant snow conditions, he usually needs sharpening up when it comes to changing his balance for changing snow conditions. By far the most prevalent fault is the failure to lean forward when going into shaded, slick snow or an icy patch.

The technique is not to "nose dive" when you come into a faster slick piece of snow, but to anticipate with a dropping of the entire body so that the normal running stance (see erect skier in illustration) becomes a lower, forward stance that shifts the weight toward the tips in anticipation of the slick spot.

The truth is that you can get your skis to catch up with you much more readily than you can catch up with them. When in doubt, drop forward.

SKI EXTRA:

Mother, May I Go Out to Ski?

by Abby Rand

No matter where I ski, I never fail to encounter the same girl, standing immobilized atop a mogul waiting for death or a hungry eagle to deliver her. Her name is always Harriet, which seems odd, particularly in German-speaking countries. Anyway, there is Harriet hung up on this mogul, and thirty feet below her stands this mean-looking guy wearing longthongs. That's how I know her name. He keeps saying, "Come on Harriet. It is *not* steep."

It *is* steep, and Harriet knows it. She also knows that if she were alone, she could discreetly sidestep, but she fears Longthongs' scorn as much as she fears the moguls. Eventually, she hurtles herself down the precipice and lands alive, but psychically scarred.

It is not Harriet's fault that she does not ski very well. Her mistake is giving in to Longthongs' determination to help her ski better. Longthongs is a Real Skier.

What Harriet should be is a follower of the separate but equal sport of Hickory Limb Skiing. Its name, its outlook and its technique stem (you should excuse the expression) from the rhyme about hanging your clothes on the hickory limb but not going near the water. (It has nothing to do with the use of hickory wood in making skis.)

That rhyme, significantly, says, "Yes, my darling daughter," not "my darling son." Hickory Limb Skiers are predominantly, but not exclusively, female.

They are people who genuinely enjoy skiing, but already ski about as well as they ever will, which is less well than most of their friends. They would ski content if left alone. But missionary zeal is rampant on the slopes. Be challenged. Improve. Bend your knees. Lean forward. Pat your head. Rub your tummy. Nag, nag, nag.

The primary goal of Hickory Limbing is to shake off unwanted assistance. The secondary goal is to ski in such a manner that is actually fun. The tertiary goal is to save face. Since all skiers are equal once their skis are off, those who can't be out-skied by day can be out-fireplaced by night.

How is it done? Schools do not teach Hickory Limb technique. Books and magazines offer aid, but only indirectly. Since it is a clandestine pursuit, no one goes around giving away advice.

I'll squeal. I happen to be an avid, and if I say so myself, an accomplished Hickory Limber. I must say so myself. I am so good nobody knows I am doing it. Here then, for the first time in visible ink, are the basic rules of the game.

Rule One: Never head for the hills in the company of real beginners. You must establish innocence-by-association. Anyway, we can assume that you want to learn Hickory Limbing for the very reason that you habitually travel with Real Skiers.

Rule Two: Start work the minute you get in the car. Advocate going to a different, more difficult mountain. Insist on getting to the mountain in time for the Milk Run. Recommend staying in spartan lodges and skipping lunch. Permit yourself, graciously, to be overruled. The point here is to establish your sincerity.

Rule Three: Dress Real. At least twenty-five per cent of your clothing and equipment must be battle-scarred. If you cannot find bamboo poles, get metal ones, but be sure the baskets are tiny. Leather mittens with ropetow marks are dandy. Forego crash helmets or racing pants with side stripes; it is unsporting to tell an out-and-out lie. Some item of your equipage should be European, imported by your own hand.

For years I carried an unpunched Davosplatz-Davosdorf bus ticket in my parka, letting it fall out at crucial moments. This meant taking off my mittens a lot, so I switched to skis clearly labelled "Sporthaus Strolz, Lech-am-Arlberg."

The object here is to look so authentic that anyone who catches you on an easy trail will assume you are helping the Ski Patrol.

Rule Four: Spend freely. Buy all-day tickets in preference to coupon books. Wearing an all-day implies that you can beat the ticket. If you buy coupons, you eventually have the problem of explaining unused stubs. Eat hearty. If you meet friends, let yourself be talked into stopping for coffee. Buying food is buying time. If ski supplies are for sale at the top of the mountain, stock up on boot laces and goggle lenses, always asking for something likely to be stashed in the back. Pay now. Ski later. When no one is looking.

Rule Five: Study. Get a trail map first thing in the morning. It is the one essential piece of Hickory Limbing equipment. Memorize where the easy trails cut into the hard ones, near the bottom. Master the unnamed connecting trails that enable you to avoid The Awful Part, but still let you be seen starting down and ending up on an Okay trail.

If you should lose your map, just follow the girls with rental skis, square-toed boots and Italian silk parkas. If *they* say a trail is difficult, you are safe.

It is hard to give specific advice without reference to a specific mountain. Since not all of us are familiar with the same areas, it will be necessary to invent one.

At Mt. Mountain, there are two chairlifts, one above the other, plus a nursery slope T-bar, which we will forget for the moment.

Under the chairs runs the Lift Line. Murder, but wide. Immediately to the left is the Death Wish (self-explanatory) and Anderl's Angst (ditto). Beyond them runs the three-mile long, sixteen-foot wide, practically uphill trail known as the Tranquilizer. There is a link between the Tranquilizer and Anderl's Angst two hundred yards above the base station. Fifty yards above it, all three trails meet.

To the right of the chairs is the Meadow (intermediate) and Lovers' Leap, which features steep shelves alternating with gentle runouts. The shelves get bumpy and icy as all get out. All get out is sound advice. Last over is the Bunny Breeze. With the exception of one interesting stretch, it is heaven.

(This is such an appealing area that I am anxious to build it. Will anyone with a million dollars and the need to establish a tax loss please get in touch?)

Okay. To avoid being over-challenged, where do you ski? Bunny Breeze? Meadow? Wrong! In the first place, you can't go around saying you have been on the Bunny Breeze and in the second place, that is the first place your friends will search when you disappear. And disappear you will, if you follow my lead.

Spend most of your time on the Tranquilizer, always cutting over to the Death Wish or Anderl's Angst at the bottom.

Stick mostly to the lower lift, since your friends will stick to the upper one.

Go to the summit at least once a day. No *après*-ski discussion is complete without a section on conditions at the top.

Be sure to ask the man at the top of the lift what the temperature is. Later, you can report that the man at the top of the lift said it was ten degrees above zero. He always does, even in April, so you are safe.

It is essential, I am afraid, to make one run down the Death Wish. I recommend 1 P.M., when everyone you know will be eating lunch.

Lovers' Leap is also a must. Here is where connecting trail expertise is handy. You can build a story around an incident on Lovers' Leap without mentioning it happened while you were climbing uphill from the Bunny Breeze cut-off.

At some point in the day, it is advisable to surface. Go to the Lift Line. Stay there until someone you know rides by on the lift. Wave. Shout. Be noticed. Then duck back to the Meadow.

Now let's get back to that nursery slope. We do not have to give it a name, since you will always refer to it as "that little thing down at the bottom." Insist on starting the day here with a few practice runs to test new boots (bindings, skis, wax, lipstick). Succumb to a few runs there right before lunch because "there's no lift line." Make it clear you want to practice an exercise you read in *SKI,* or to teach a friend. If you don't have a friend who will submit to teaching, pick one up.

No matter how well you hide, you are bound to run into Real Skiers you know sooner or later. If they ask where you have been, point in the direction of the Death Wish and say "On the whatzis."

If asked about conditions, say, "It is icy in the middle, but good on the sides." This satisfactorily describes ninety-eight per cent of all probable conditions, ninety-eight per cent of the time. Moreover, it implies you took it straight down the shoulder of the trail.

If you get stuck skiing with them, here are some useful strategems.

Start downhill with your friends, but let them get ahead (easy). Then, when you catch up, say you had to loosen your binding. At the next steep pitch, say you had to tighten your binding. Then on to the boots. Tighten. Loosen. Tighten. Loosen. Maintain a steady rhythm.

Variations: runny noses, near-accidents, encounters with long-lost brothers, pauses to admire the sun dancing on the icicles.

By all means, take along a camera. When all else fails, insist on taking everyone's picture. Irresistible.

Desperation Maneuver A: Duck over to another trail, wait for Them in the lift line. Place hands on hips and say, "What kept you?"

Desperation Maneuver B: Hide behind a tree, until the Enemy goes on. Do two runs to their three. End up ahead of them. As they approach behind you, shove off, shouting over your shoulder, "Shift your weight more. Lean forward."

A full day of activity is vital. Be the last one off the mountain, even if it means curtailing your lunch break at 4:05 P.M., in order to make the last ride uphill.

Judicious use of refreshment facilities cannot be overemphasized.

This brings us to Europe, a continent created for the Hickory Limber. Those sun-drenched terraces! Those exotic drinks! Those fascinating opportunities to improve your French and German and learn about their way of life! (Their way of life is sitting on those sun-drenched terraces, drinking exotic drinks and improving your French and German, but not everybody back home knows that yet.)

In Europe, the mountains are bigger. Even without trees, it is easier to hide. On an alp, a thorough map-reading can win you not thirty minutes but a whole day of Freedom from Friends.

Ski with the locals, if possible. Remember it is a large world, and the neighbors will never know.

When you return to your native hills, the conversational possibilities will be endless. Few Americans understand that there are Alps and alps, some of them quite easy.

To protect your rear, avoid the European resorts most frequently skied by Americans. Return with glowing, and unverifiable tales of your feats at Malga Zirago, Engelberg or Wörgl.

Since Real Skiing will grow and human nature will remain constant, I predict that Hickory Limb Skiing is in for a boom. If nothing else, it represents a tangible advance in the war between the sexes, ski troops division. Men who would hesitate to lead a lady up the garden path, think nothing of leading her down Anderl's Angst. While the latter is not a fate worse than death, it might well be tantamount.

If you love life more than skiing itself, Hickory Limbing provides a pleasant principle for survival—if you can't lick 'em, don't join 'em.

V. *Advanced Intermediate Class*

The only final form for Class D of the American system is the stem christie. It can be approached by the stem garland exercise. This exercise is designed to prepare the skier for the sliding movement that follows the closing of the legs from the stem position. Here is the essence of the stem christie. In effect, a stem is combined with the uphill christie studied in Class C. The real kick of the stem christie turn, however, comes later, when the skier learns to close the skis early in the turn.

Stem Garland

The stem garland is designed to aid skiers by learning to open and close the skis with smooth fluid movements and to end the turn by side-slipping and resetting edges. The garland cycle is repeated several times in a row before stopping.

Beginning Stem Christie

The beginning stem christie holds the stem into the fall line (sixth figure from top). Skis close coming out of fall line (seventh figure). Skier sets edges with down motion (last figure) to finish the turn in the new traverse.

Advanced Stem Christie

The final form definition: from the traverse, the uphill ski is stemmed with an accompanying down motion. With an up motion, the weight is transferred to the stemmed outside ski. The inside ski is brought parallel and advanced as the skis enter the christie phase. The body assumes angulation as the outside shoulder gradually is brought back. The edges are reset with a down motion to finish the turn in the new traverse.

Advanced stem christie analysis: ski is stemmed (second figure from the top) and accompanying down motion is plain. Up-unweighting occurs in third figure, weight is changed to stemmed ski, and unweighted inside ski is brought alongside and advanced. By the fourth figure, when skier is in fall line, the skis are together and both angulation and bringing back of the outside shoulder are evident. Down motion in fifth figure sets edges to finish turn. Down motion and stemming for the second turn occur in eighth figure. Edges set to finish at bottom.

SKI POINTERS FOR THE ADVANCED INTERMEDIATE CLASS

Think Ahead

by Bob Savard, Certified, USEASA; Member, PSIA

To make correct stem christie turns through the fall line requires a number of coordinated movements: switching the lead ski, shifting the weight and changing the edges, all requiring changes in body positioning. It is difficult, however, to try to think of all these details at once. A better approach is to *think ahead to the end of the turn rather than to lose your natural coordination and timing by trying to remember too many details during the turn itself*. Practice concentrating on sliding into the position where the skis close and become parallel at the end of the turn (see upper figure in illustration). Develop an image of what your body position will be at the end of the turn; the many details to be accomplished in the turn itself will come with more rhythm and ease. Thinking ahead gives you the timing necessary for varied terrain and snow conditions.

FALL LINE

A Gentle Brushing

by Georgia Hotton, Certified, SRMSIA

In modern skiing, the recreational skier has begun to rely more and more on a sharp heel thrust to do the short swing turn down the fall line. With the use of a sharp heel thrust, you can manage a rather competent short swing on smooth hard-packed slopes. But if this is the only way you know how to short swing, then you are in trouble in almost any other snow condition. For instance, in heavy snow or through moguls the sharp heel thrust can lead to a wobbly, uncertain descent.

To steady up in heavy snow or in moguls, you will have to learn to gentle that heel thrust, to float your turn rather than force it.

To tame your heel thrust into a gentle, light swing, emphasize steering the tips of the skis around the turn, particularly the tip of the outside ski. De-emphasize, in your mind, the skidding of the tails of the skis. Keep your skis fairly flat (see illustration) and set your edges as lightly as possible at the end of the swing. Follow this with the unweighting and then float your skis through the next turn.

You'll find your skiing immeasurably easier when you tame that heel thrust a bit.

Push the Turn

by Mike Savell, Certified, PNSIA; Member, PSIA

When the intermediate skier goes from stem turns to stem christies, he finds that his turns are no longer "steered"; rather, they become "controlled skids." For many intermediates, this presents a problem, for skidding is different than the movements previously learned. As a result, the intermediate skier often tries to "bank" his way around the turn; that is, he gets going fast and, to get the skis skidding around, leans inward, banking his whole body. This is "overbanking." When a skier overbanks, it is an attempt to "pull" the skis around. Overbanking leads to a fall. The primary use of banking should be to maintain balance at high speeds, not to supply turning power. The right way to skid a ski involves something quite different. In the American Technique, *the skid is accomplished by pushing the heels of the skis sideways, toward the outside of the turn.* It is much better to use a heel thrust for turning power. This vigorous push should be accompanied by increased comma (bend at the waist) for balance. (See illustration.) The stem skier needs lots of work on heel thrust.

Follow Through with Ankle Bend

by Bill Roth, Certified, FWSIA

Most skiers start their turns with fairly good ankle action, but as the turn progresses, they lose their forward ankle lean until, at the end of the turn, their legs from the knee down are straight. The resulting knee bend without ankle bend puts them in the familiar sitting position in which it is difficult for the tails of the skis to skid. This, in turn, results in loss of control at the finish of each turn and is the reason why so many skiers pick up unwanted speed after two or three linked turns.

With proper ankle bend at the end of a turn, the body weight is kept over the feet. The skier is standing ready for action and can immediately come up forward and down again in unweighting for the following turn. Without ankle bend, the weight is behind the feet and the skier must readjust his position before he can start the next turn. In linking short or quick turns, you can see where one would lose the proper timing needed for polished, fluid turns.

So, say to yourself, over and over, ankle bend at the end of each turn. Before long, this will be one of your good skiing habits.

Correct Hand Position

by Don Henderson, Certified, USEASA; Member, PSIA

The position of the hands is vital to a correct body position over the skis. To achieve this, simply extend the hands forward to a relaxed position alongside the skis—do not reach out in front of you. Reaching out will make the arms go stiff. Raise the ski pole tips enough to clear the snow and point them to the rear, keeping the tips about one foot off the snow. *The hand position should simulate a pair of hands holding a huge horizontally-set steering wheel.* Hands in front and arms relaxed describe the best position of the hands at all times except in the traverse positions. In traversing, the "steering wheel" position of the hands is turned thirty to forty degrees down the hill (see illustration). If you keep the hands "on the wheel," two important things will happen: you will lean forward and your weight will be over the downhill ski. Above all, you will be assured of good balance at all times.

Anchor the Head

by Jim Snobble, Certified, RMSIA; Member, PSIA

A problem that bothers many beginning and intermediate skiers (some experts as well) is the tendency to move the head to the inside of the turn. Too much of this sideward motion with the head, either to initiate or complete the turn, will invariably place too much weight on the inside ski of the turn. There is an analogy or lesson to be learned here from the sport of golf. Those skiers who also play golf know that one of the cardinal sins in a golf swing is to sway the head to one side. The same principle applies in skiing. As the head is the anchor of the swing in golf, so in skiing the head is the anchor for correct body position over the skis. The comma position emphatically requires that your head stay over the skis even though your hips are to the inside of the turn (see illustration). So remember, if you will *keep your head anchored over the skis,* you will find your weight stays where it should stay—on the outside ski.

VI. *Advanced Class*

Here we are at the step where the skier learns to minimize the stem movement and to maximize the sliding movement of the stem christie—the parallel turn. The goal is to make sure that the "residual stem" is completely removed, and that the skier's mind does not even think stem, but substitutes unweighting. Instead of stemming, unweighting becomes the key to bringing the skis around. Unweighting reduces friction between skis and snow to a minimum, enabling the lower body to swivel the skis to the new direction. The lower body turn is accelerated by an opposite counter turn in the upper body. This "countering" supplies the force with which it is possible to start the skis turning.

Parallel Christie

From the traverse, the edge of the downhill ski is set with a down motion. With an up motion, the weight is transferred to the outside ski and the edge is changed. The inside ski is advanced. Turning power is applied. The body assumes angulation as the outside shoulder is gradually brought back. Edges are reset with a down motion to finish the turn in the new traverse.

Natural Positioning

Every position can be exaggerated. One of the results of exaggeration is loss of balance. And by twisting or tipping the body leg muscles are forced to strain under the weight. The American system emphasizes natural position. It insists that the skeletal structure should carry the weight of the skier. The skier should use no more of the reverse shoulder motion than is needed to make the turn. This leaves him in a rather relaxed position, ready to adjust to the terrain or snow. The skier who exaggerates the reverse is vulnerable to changes in terrain. In the twisted position he has assumed, he cannot move quickly to make the small balance corrections necessary.

Parallel Christie with Check

The most effective substitute for the stem is not just an up motion which gets the weight off the skis but an up motion preceded by a check, or heel thrust. The effect is to form the so-called "platform" on which the skier makes his up motion more quickly and decisively than he could without the check.

How to do the parallel christie with check: from the traverse, the skier begins a sideslip as though for an uphill christie. Then, as the tails of his skis begin to slide out, he drops his body, increases angulation and plants his pole. This sharp drop sets the edges of the skis very firmly into the snow, giving the skier a strong platform from which he can push off vigorously into the unweighting phase of the turn.

After the Platform, What?

by Ernie McCulloch, Certified, CSIA

In good, tight parallel skiing there is an imprint left in the snow before each turn which results from "edge set or bite." Edge set is one of the secrets of sound parallel skiing. It is most pronounced when speed is held to a minimum on a steep slope by strong check turns. Each edge set creates a "platform" from which you can lift into the next turn.

Many pupils do not understand what should happen to the body after the platform is set. Action stills of expert skiers show that the phase

occurring after edge set and at the beginning of the subsequent turn is a balanced stance called "neutral position." As the skis are released from the edge set and move toward the fall line, the body is practically square over the skis for a split second. Your body is in full balance and ready to react at any moment. Most skiers hurry too much into the new turn.

In teaching, I emphasize the neutral position by having pupils coast down the fall line in the neutral position after the edge set and unweighting, thus forcing a balanced position. Gradually I let pupils speed up timing and cut down the duration of the neutral position until it is held for only a split second before edging into the new turn.

In the pictures below, the neutral position is obvious. Both my arms are held out to the side, giving me a strongly balanced position.

PARALLEL TURNS ILLUSTRATED (Top to bottom, right to left.) (1) Modified traverse position shows tails of skis starting downhill in preparation for the edge set. (2) The shoulders and hips reverse. Knees push forward. Pole is brought forward, ready for edge set. (3) Skis come around to almost right angle with fall line. The knees bend and tilt into the hill giving the edges of the skis a set in the snow. Pole is planted. (4) Skier hops. Knees straighten. Tails of the skis lift. Body is becoming square to the skis. (5) The neutral position. Tails of the skis contact snow. Body is square to the skis. Arms extend for balance. The knees are at medium bend. (6) Knees push forward. Tails swivel across fall line. Upper body reverses and takes comma position. The edges of the skis take grip in the snow. (7) Turn continues with forward pressure of the knees. Outside arm and pole come forward to plant pole for the next edge set. Upper body is tilting slightly downhill.

SKI POINTERS FOR THE ADVANCED CLASS

Change the Lead

by Wally Abersold, Certified, ISIA; Member, PSIA

There are two rules for knowing which ski is to lead the other in proper ski technique.

The first rule is: uphill ski ahead. This means that whenever you are traversing, the uphill ski leads—by about a half-boot length.

The second rule supersedes the first: whenever you are in a turn, the inside ski leads. Of course, in an uphill turn from a traverse, there is no problem, as the same ski leads. But in a downhill turn, a lead change is necessary.

The sooner you can change lead in the turn, the better. If the uphill ski is brought back at the very start of the turn, as you unweight or stem, then you will get a nice smooth arc. Also, you won't cross your tips. Reasons: pulling the outside ski of the turn back makes it easier to get your weight on the outside ski correctly, and centrifugal force won't be able to force the tip of the inside ski across the outside tip.

Sometimes an early lead change is all that stands between a good skier and really good skiing.

Squeeze the Knees

by Roger Claude Gaudin, Certified, CSIA

Sometimes the only thing lacking in a parallel skier is that little extra togetherness of the legs. Besides appearance, having the legs close together through the turn improves steadiness and edging.

Try this: stand with your skis a foot or so apart. (Top illustration.) Then, without hopping, bring both skis together. Sustain this tightening effort after your skis have met. Squeeze the knees. (Bottom illustration.)

Now, apply it while you make your turns, with particular emphasis on the start of the turn where many skiers have a little stem motion they are not aware of.

With practice, this "squeezing the knees" will become automatic, and your style and steadiness will improve considerably.

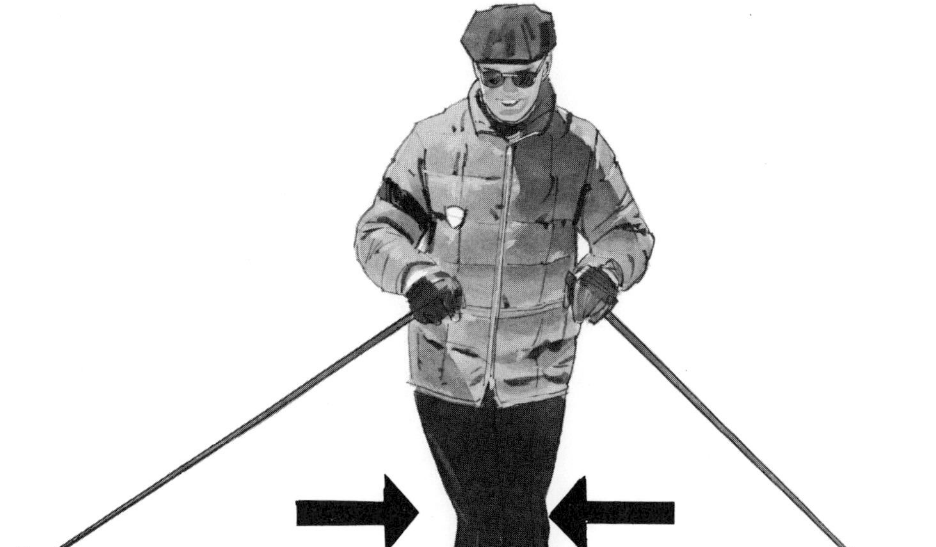

Arm Circle

by Joe Auckenthaler, Certified, FWSIA; Member, PSIA

There is a simple but nevertheless very important pointer in the way that a good parallel skier finishes his parallel turn. He finishes it with an "extension" or up movement in preparation for the next turn and, in this final extension movement, he rotates his upper body in the direction of the next turn. So, think of circling your uphill arm and shoulder in the direction of the new turn (see arrow) rather than of the up movement. *In other words, to get a smoother transition to the next turn, you should concentrate on the circling motion you make with the upper body.* This may be the very thing that you have been lacking in your technique for making consecutive parallel turns come off smoothly. Don't over-exaggerate the circular movement, however, because it will lead to mambo-type skiing in a situation where mambo is not wanted.

Leaning Out Is In

by Hans Georg, Certified, FWSIA

Regardless of the method of teaching either modern Austrian or American technique, the comma position is *the* most important body position in teaching. It is used when traversing, it is used when trying to hold on icy slopes and it is used when setting edges for the bounce up to the next turn. It is used in exaggerated manner (see illustration) when trying for fast sharp turns, when in tight series of slalom gates and in the wedeln. To achieve a good stable comma position, then, is very important. The best way to teach yourself to hold a comma is to concentrate on leaning *outward* (see arrow) from the turn or the traverse with the upper body. Many people have been taught to think of leaning their hips in to turn, but this may result in weighting the inside ski. On the other hand, *by emphasizing the out-lean of the shoulders and upper body the outside ski of the turn is automatically weighted, and the hips naturally take their proper position.* So, avoid telling yourself to incline the hip to the inside, for you will be concentrating on the wrong part of the body. Your best approach is to think of "leaning out" from the turn. In this way, you will not get caught with your weight on the uphill ski. Your weight will stay outside and downhill to give the control you need.

Pick Up for Parallel Turns

by Marcel Barel, Certified, FWSIA; Member, PSIA

To set a smoother parallel than you have, you probably need some more weight on that outside ski. The best and simplest exercise for learning weight shift and balance is a long, slow turn with the inside ski lifted off the snow.

Here's the correct way to do it: start in the fall line of a very gentle slope. Pick up a little speed and choose a smooth spot for a left or right turn. Before (not after) starting the turn, pick up the inside ski, leaving the tip of the ski on the snow.

Complete the turn without setting the ski down. Try to press the boot of the inside ski against the outside boot through the turn.

When you can do this one-ski turn with confidence, you will have all the tools for a perfect parallel turn.

No-pole Turns

by Murdo MacDonald, Certified, USEASA

Even though beginners should be encouraged to use the poles to help them turn, inevitably there comes the point where the skier has to stop for a bit and concentrate on eliminating the pole habits that form unconsciously. These habits are habits of overuse. Even the advanced skier typically thrusts his pole into the snow too hard and typically leans on the pole as he swings around a turn (instead of pushing off from the pole to initiate the turn). Then there is the skier who uses the pole as a crutch, dragging it in the snow or jabbing away at the snow as he goes through the turn.

There is a way to test whether you are overthrusting or leaning, dragging or jabbing: make a few turns on easy terrain without using your poles at all. This quickly shows up any errors of overusing the pole; it quickly demonstrates whether you are using your legs properly to supply the lift for a parallel turn and whether you are staying on the outside ski during a stem turn. A few runs without poles will help you to stay on top of your skis, improve your balance and make you realize that a good skier can ski easily without poles. He uses his poles sparingly on normal terrain.

Sensing a Scissor

by Les Outzs, Certified, ISIA; Member, PSIA

A common fault of the parallel skier is scissoring. Since the ski is wider at the front than under the foot, whenever we fail to keep the outside ski weighted and the inside ski at the same angle to the snow, the inside ski takes over and hooks uphill, causing an unsightly open-knees look.

One way of eliminating the error is to become conscious of it. The reason we don't correct it is that we are not aware of the beginning of the problem.

So, go out on a slope and start a slow forward sideslip. Deliberately put pressure on the upper ski. You will find that the tip climbs uphill (see illustration), and the tails may eventually cross.

Now, correct your position; weight to the lower ski, upper ski at the same angle to the snow as the lower. The skis and knees stay together. If you can keep the difference in mind, you will eliminate scissoring.

Look at That Track

by Erik Lessing, Certified, SRMSIA

You can ski for years without actually thinking about whether or not you are making longer, graceful turns. The most advantageous time to analyze your parallel turn is after a light snowfall. This gives you a chance to see what you have done. First of all, your track should be a smooth curve. If the edge of the track is ragged, it means you are over-edging all through the turn. (The skis should have maximum edge only at the end of the turn.) Second: how wide is the turn? *If the track is narrow (see skier left in illustration) then you are carving a nice long turn. Don't make a turn any shorter than it has to be.* If it is a wide track (*see skier to right*), it indicates that you are spinning the skis into the new direction too fast for most purposes. You are getting a wide, skidding, sliding turn when you don't need one. Naturally, ski tails slide a little in any turn, but a wide track means that you are slashing through your turn too abruptly to make a long, smooth turn. Try this exercise with two other skiers: practice turning to the traverse line from a given point in the middle of a slope. The skier with the narrowest track from fall line to traverse line is the most graceful.

Proper Pole Handling

by Dick Sexe, Certified, CUSSA

The crux of good pole handling is using the pole to give a helping lift to the skier at the point at which the skier unweights in the turn; thereafter the pole should be handled so as not to hinder the turn by hanging the skier up.

The best way to make sure that the pole is available at the right time and out of the way thereafter is to pronate. Pronation is very simple. When the pole goes in, the thumb points up. The skier gets an instant of lift from the pole. Then the thumb pronates, that is, points across the body, and the hand is kept forward, as in the illustration.

If the pole is not pronated, the pole hand tends to be carried behind the elbow, the skier will tend to be set back on his heel, and his weight will tend to go on the wrong (inside) ski.

Practicing this motion in dry dock might help. Plant the pole on a down motion (of the knees) and as you come up from the down position, pronate the pole into the forward position. Do it with the other pole and then do it alternately. This is the vital rhythm of the hands and arms in a series of linked turns.

Pole Upward

by Dick Georgi, Certified, USEASA

One of the biggest problems of skiing is the mistiming of the pole plant. Most of the skiers who come unstrung through faulty pole action don't know it: they blame the hill. But the right pole action is fairly simple to perform, even though it's hard to spot a fault, particularly in yourself.

The timing of the pole plant is thus: the pole is put into the snow with a straight downward action just as the up motion begins.

Eight skiers out of ten plant too early, before the lift for the turn has started. This means that they are over-depending on the pole as a means of turning. The pole is an aid. If it is put into the snow too early it hangs up and throws you.

Just for the practice of it, run down a gentle fall line pushing the pole in as you make a lift—don't make any turns at first. (See arrows in illustration.)

Next, go down the fall line making small hop turns, planting the pole *after* the up motion. You'll see that your style has become sophisticated and light, instead of heavy and hard.

Hammer It Home

by Dieter Nohl, Certified, USEASA

The art of the sudden stop is, in part, pole work. Skiers who like to take it fast are often faced with the need for a quick brake, the quicker the better.

The wrong way is to make a sharp uphill turn and try to jam to a stop with the skis alone.

The right way is to turn sharply, edge hard and then come hammering down on the outside pole (see illustration).

Not only will the pole help you stop sooner but it will help pin you down, so that the force generated by the sudden turn doesn't throw you over sideways onto the very object you were trying to avoid.

The art of hammering in the pole should not be learned at the moment of an emergency. Go out on the slope and make five or six really quick stops from increasingly high speeds, getting the pole in at the very instant your turn has ended.

The properly executed stop christie can keep you out of all sorts of unwelcome spots.

Touch and Go

by Denis Tremblay, Certified, CUSSA, CSIA

Studying the habits of beginning parallel skiers, the objective observer is inclined to note that a good number of them want to sneak their skis around the turn without unweighting. They stick a pole in the snow and hang on it, trying to swing around it like a monkey on a flag pole.

The best way to get the pole-hangers off the habit is to introduce them to the touch-and-go exercise.

In this exercise, the skier runs down the fall line of a gentle slope and sinks toward the snow to put the pole into the snow. As he puts the pole in, he gives a good high hop straight up in the air (see illustration). This teaches him: (1) to get off the snow in preparation for the turn; (2) not to depend too much on the pole.

The skier should practice this exercise until he can go down the fall line hopping easily, depending on his legs to spring him off the ground, not the pole.

When he now goes back to parallel, he takes the hop with him. To start the turn, he hops and swings his skis. As a matter of fact, he is likely to have made some shallow parallel turns during the hop exercise because he will naturally change his direction a bit each time he comes down.

SKI EXTRA:

Budget Tips for the Ski Weekend

by Karin Gottlieb

FIFTEEN TIPS FOR THE FAMILY

1. *Transportation:* Consider skiing in the purchase of your next car. Station wagons and bus-type vehicles can be economical on gas, and many models are now equipped for camping or sleeping. If the car you're buying will be your all-purpose car, then obviously the pick-up truck with an attached camper unit would be out of the question. (Who wants to go rolling off to a dinner engagement in a pick-up truck?) If however, you are in a position to purchase something along these lines, its uses are manifold and not limited to skiing.

2. *Save Phone Calls:* A single long distance call to the area's accommodations booking center can save you a lot in the long run. Even if you know the lodge, and the owner is your brother—if they're full, they're full. The central booking agency can save you several phone calls and will usually be able to find you the accommodations you need.

3. *Farmhouses, Motels:* If you're prepared to eschew the luxuries of the larger, more elaborate ski lodges, the private home or farmhouse-type accommodation will save you money. It's usually comfortable and quiet—and who wants the kids hanging around the bar all night, anyway? Locate these places during summer travels if you're in the area or consult the area's accommodations center. Many areas also have housekeeping cabins or motel units with cooking facilities. If food is bought at home, the cost for weekend eating is no greater than if the family stayed home.

4. *Extra Beds:* Take a folding cot or travel bed for children. If you can set it up in your room, or put all the children in one room, it cuts down costs.

5. *Rent a House?* If you're going to all the fuss and bother of traveling about with your own food and your own beds, why not set up your

own headquarters at your favorite ski area? There are many points which must be considered, however, before one gaily assumes that this arrangement would be perfect. Unless your family is large and you spend every weekend and school vacation skiing, the cost may be prohibitive. On the other hand, it can work well if you're willing to share with another family, alternating weekends and vacations. All of you together may be a vast mistake. (Then again, it may not be.)

6. *Buy Real Estate?* If you like the area well enough and spend enough time there, consider building or buying your own weekend house. A strategic location can result in accessibility to three of four ski areas. With this variety, the location ought to appeal for years—enough to make the initial investment worthwhile. Select an area which offers summer vacation use as well. But again, weigh the pros and cons carefully before going ahead. Ask yourself these questions: Will you use it in the summer? Can it be considered an investment? (Land at many ski areas is multiplying in value.) Should you build a new house? Is it possible to buy and renovate an old farmhouse? How much will you utilize it? Remember that the average American skier skis only twelve days a year.

7. *Equipment Pool:* A neighborhood buying and selling pool saves on equipment for children who often outgrow skis, boots and poles before they wear them out. If you live near ski country, most homes have at least a couple of pairs of spare boots "that Junior has outgrown, and

we're waiting for Susie to grow into." Check your local ski club to see if they sponsor such a pool. Possibly the child's school does. If there's no pool organized, but you think the field looks promising, organize your own. Simply set aside a cellar for a Saturday in November and invite the neighbors to bring along their children's ski equipment.

8. *What Kind of Area?* Pick your area carefully before embarking on a weekend or vacation. Decide whether you will settle for a T-bar or rope tow area to shave the price of uphill transportation. If you want to go to a chairlift area, expect lift ticket prices to be higher. Smaller areas are generally less crowded and you may get more skiing for less money.

9. *Family Season Tickets:* Some areas have family ski plans which (among other benefits) entitle one to lower lift rates (about ten per cent). Others have family season passes at considerable savings if you're doing much skiing. Membership in organized skiing may also entitle you to lower lift rates at some areas.

10. *Protect Against Theft:* Families and single skiers can save money in the long run by protecting their equipment from theft. Use the available storage facilities (lockers, ski locks) that most areas offer. Many ski racks for cars now come with built-in locks; if you don't have one, a simple padlock can be used. The extra expense is worth it.

11. *Waxing:* Wax your own skis. Cold wax is good enough for average skiing, average snow. Hot wax, if necessary, can be prepared over a Sterno stove.

12. *Touring:* Cross-country touring, while involving the initial cost of adjustable bindings, presents no other additional costs. It's away from the stamping hordes; it opens up whole new vistas of previously unseen territory and affords a glimpse of wildlife. In the age of fast lifts, well-groomed slopes and the urge to schuss, cross-country touring can be a pleasantly relaxing variation for the whole family.

13. *Children's Lift Tickets:* Don't waste the cost of a day ticket on a small child, one who is just beginning to ski or one who feels the cold easily. They'll be better off with individual ride tickets and, in the case of the cold children, much happier. They'll feel free to go in the warming hut more frequently. A certain amount of climbing will also keep children physically fit, warm and will save on the cost of tickets besides.

14. *Insurance:* Should one of your family be injured, expenses and worry can be saved if you've taken the precaution to be covered by ski accident insurance. The United States Ski Association (Hotel Broad-

moor, Colorado Springs, Colo.) offers this type of insurance at reasonable premium rates.

15. *Conditioning:* Injuries can be avoided if the whole family participates in a pre-season conditioning program. After sitting in school all week, children are as vulnerable as desk-bound adults. Ski carefully. Quit when you're tired.

FIFTEEN MONEY SAVERS FOR THE SINGLE SKIER

1. *For Beginners:* If you're a beginner, don't worry about getting to that glamorous, far-off ski resort yet. The closer, less sophisticated areas will do until you get your skis under you. Then you can get your money's worth of enjoyment when you travel to the big name areas. Also, rent your equipment until you are sure you like the sport. In many instances, the rental fee can be applied toward the purchase of your own equipment.

2. *Skiing Vacation:* Consider a winter vacation. A whole week of skiing (even if not a learn-to-ski week) can cost less than three weekend trips—less money, less travel time, less wear-and-tear on you.

3. *Single Area:* Consider skiing one area all winter. It can cost less than if you switch areas every weekend. You can buy a season pass and you'll become familiar with one town's characteristics, costs and people.

4. *Food:* Make your own lunches—but know your area. Some places frown on "brown-baggers," others set aside a special place in the

warming hut for those who bring their own lunch. A word of warning: buy your food before you come. Resort prices sometimes approximate those of a gold rush town. Don't leave food to freeze in the car on a very cold day. If everything works out well, you can save money and avoid the line at the cafeteria.

5. *Join a Ski House?* Joining a ski club or an informal group of friends who are looking to rent a lodge on a seasonal basis at an area may be an advantage. But there are many angles to consider. Your lodging and food costs are cut appreciably if the group is large enough. Even *après*-ski costs are diminished with the probability of Saturday evening parties right at your lodge. Still, if it's going to cost you one hundred dollars to join the ski house, this amount is equivalent to twenty-five nights at four dollars in a lodge, or a total of twelve weekends. Are you going to ski this much? Weigh all points. Examine what you're getting for the price. Some summer homes—with no insulation and poor heating—are rented at exorbitant fees. You may be more comfortable in a lodge.

6. *Ski Bum on Weekends:* Many lodges increase their staff on weekends to handle the larger crowds. This arrangement usually takes care of room and board, if not lift tickets or a pass (usually only the full-time ski bum gets a pass).

7. *Dormitories:* If you're looking for less expensive lodgings, consider the dormitories. They are not as costly as more elaborate lodges, and they provide a "get acquainted" atmosphere for the single skier. Many lodges have several rooms set aside for dormitory-style quarters.

8. *Sleeping Bag:* Your initial investment in a sleeping bag can be recovered by enabling you to obtain less expensive dormitory lodgings or even to camp out on friends' sofas. An air mattress is an added expense, but added comfort. Both items can also be used for summer camping.

9. *Ski Lessons:* Generally, beginner classes do not utilize the lifts. Don't spend money on day tickets or a book of individual rides until you discover what the requirements for your class will include.

10. *Individual Lift Ride vs. A-Day Ticket:* Attempt to figure in advance how much skiing you will do in a day—then calculate if the number of individual lift rides involved would cost less than a day ticket. You can also check on areas that offer half-day tickets.

11. *Bus Tours:* Bus tours, running anywhere from thirty dollars and up per person, include transportation, lodging and most meals. Some tours take their own instructors, but check to determine if these instructors are as competent as those employed by the area. Some areas (particularly in the East) don't welcome tour groups. You yourself have to decide whether or not you want to spend the weekend with a possibly uncongenial tour group. A less restricted, yet economical, variation is the bus which takes the skier to the area but doesn't tie him tightly to a tour. Bus transportation offers a safety factor which is worth considering if you've ever made the Sunday night trip home drooping with sleep and driving on an icy road.

12. *Automobiles and Car Pools:* If you drive yourself, consider a small economy car. AAA figures, developed in 1961 by Runzheimer and

Co. in the Chicago area, show a definitely lower operating cost for domestic and foreign compacts. On the basis of ten thousand miles driven annually, total annual costs for the domestic compact would be $248 less than for a standard car; for the foreign car $536 less.

If you have no car, try to get in a car pool. Some car owners merely elect to charge their riders for gas and oil. But a fairer arrangement for the owner is payment on a basis that covers not only these costs, but also maintenance, depreciation, tires, insurance, etc. AAA figures allow $621 yearly for depreciation on a (fairly) new standard car; tire and theft insurance, $30; liability $117; license and registration $23.60; all totaling $792 in *fixed costs* per year. This averages out to $2.17 per day.

The *variable costs* include gas and oil at 2.6¢ average per mile, maintenance at .7¢ per mile and tires at .4¢ per mile for a total of 3.7¢ per mile. Variable plus fixed costs come to 11¢ per mile. Therefore, a fair way to figure costs is:

$$\frac{\textit{Total distance x 11¢ + tolls}}{\textit{Number of persons (driver included)}} = \textit{cost per person}$$

On a typical weekend trip of four hundred miles, including $5 in tolls, costs would total $49. For five passengers, the cost per person would be $9.80, still well below public transportation costs. Toll costs—running as high as $5–$6 per weekend trip in some sections of the country—can be avoided entirely by taking regular routes rather than toll expressways and thruways. A handy booklet, *Your Driving Costs,* can be obtained from the American Automobile Association, 1712 G Street, N.W., Washington 6, D.C.

13. *Hitchhike:* If not from your home point (chancy these days), you may at least hitchhike from the lodge to the mountain. At ski areas, it's even respectable for girls to do so.

14. *Use Bulletin Boards at Lodge or Area:* Many single skiers with room in the car will take passengers for little more than gas and oil costs. This is not, strictly speaking, a car pool, since it's generally a one-time trip. Still, many motorists appreciate the company enough to accommodate you at a very low cost. Bulletin boards are also handy to check

for used equipment. And should you break one ski, don't spend money on a whole new pair before trying to locate a mate via the bulletin board.

15. *The Going-Home Supper:* An increasing number of lodges will willingly provide the home-bound skier with a box lunch to take on the trip back. The expense of eating on the way home is reduced, and the time you would spend stopping for something to eat is totally eliminated.

VII. *Expert Class*

Here we are on expert ground at last. The wedeln is the ultimate turn in normal skiing. Although no skier can truly be called expert until he can perform the wedeln on expert terrain, the turn itself, or rather the turns themselves (wedeln turns are always linked in series) are definitely expert manuevers. Basically, wedeln compresses the parallel turn. The timing of the up motion, pole handling, counter movement and angulation become critical. A mistake throws the whole series off. But success in connecting one wedeln turn (wedeln is Austrian for wagging) to another and another produces the graceful ballet-like series of weaving arcs that is the reward of the faithful and ambitious skier.

Single Wedeln Turn

All turns are initiated by "total motion," that is, moving the entire weight of the body to start the turn, followed by continuous motion as the body moves through the turn.

Wedeln

The wedeln consists of consecutive parallel christies without traverse.

Analysis of wedeln (shown on opposite page): elimination of traverse between turns makes for serpentine track down the fall line. Edge set and pole plant are easily seen in second figure (from top), together with the rapid down motion with which the edges are set, as in parallel, with check. Up-unweighting is shown by third figure. In fourth figure, the skier has already started down motion and begun to set the edges. In fifth figure, he has made pole plant for third turn. Up motion in sixth figure is followed by down motion of seventh; and up motion of eighth by the down motion and edge-setting of the last figure.

Wedeln from Above

Wedeln is a smooth, snakelike motion in which the skis are kept almost flat on the snow. The tails are brushed from side to side by leg action, the body being kept almost motionless and used as a stabilizing mass for the leg movements. During wedeln, the legs are gently contracted and extended just sufficiently to permit the skis to travel beneath the skier's body in a side-to-side motion. Almost all of this action takes place in the knees and ankles. The upper body always faces down the fall line, and the poles are planted with the minimum amount of hand and arm movement. As a cat stalks its prey, so does a skier execute wedeln, perhaps the most graceful maneuver in skiing.

Check Hop Garland

This exercise is designed to increase the ability of the skier to make quick successive lifts and slides so that he can use them for his wedeln. The skier starts in a medium-steep traverse, slides his tails downward, checks, then hops the tails up (middle figure, opposite page) and slides them downward again to repeat the exercise.

SKI POINTERS FOR THE EXPERT CLASS

Hands Up

by Don Schwartz, Certified, CUSSA; Member, PSIA

Aside from racing, where it is a necessity, the "up" hand position is coming more and more into use in recreational skiing; rightly, because it gives the skier a better chance to balance.

The fairly high hand position should be practiced by any skier who wants to be able to run through changing terrain with a mimimum of halts.

As shown in the illustration, the position is not rigid: the poles hang loosely, ready for planting to start a turn or to maintain balance.

While it is not good for a skier to keep picking at that snow, it is good for him to have the poles ready for a quick save in case the terrain kicks the skis the wrong way for him.

As a practice measure, take a straight run through the roughest stretch of an open slope—do not turn until you get going fairly fast and have space to make a sweeping arc. You will find that holding the hands high and loose makes it possible to run through moguls and bad spots and come out in control. The better skier tends to ski through the rough places and turn in the smooth rather than to try to turn where turning is tough.

Weight Move for Short Turns

by Hans Palmer, Certified, USEASA; Member, PSIA

The skier who has learned to make long parallel turns when he skis on shallow pitches often finds he has a difficult time switching to shorter parallel turns. The core of the problem is that in the conventional long parallel turns it is necessary to get the weight forward of the boots. This weight distribution causes the skis to carve rather than to sideslip, which is fine for long turns. But, to make short turns the skis have to sideslip more and carve less. Therefore, *the skier who is trying to shorten his turn to the degree required in wedeln must bring the weight back at least as far back as the ball of the foot* (*see arrow in illustration*) so that the skis sideslip rather than carve. This new weight distribution will cut the arc of the turn almost in half, allowing the skier to make the series of quick, linked wedeln turns necessary for steep-incline skiing. The shorter the arc, the quicker the turn, the firmer the control.

Rhythm Makes Wedeln

by John Carson, Certified, PNSIA; Member, PSIA

If you have not yet been able to make a satisfactory wedeln run, here is a way of helping you get your wedeln going. The secret is rhythm. To gain the proper rhythm for wedeln, take one step at a time. Start with a gentle slope, skis parallel and the arms well forward, almost shoulder high. *At a slow speed, begin a down-up-down motion to lift the tails of the skis off the snow about four inches (see illustration)*. Add touching of the poles to the snow on the down motion. Do not turn the skis yet. After the rhythm develops for a straight run, start sliding the tails of the skis slightly to the right (about six inches) on one hop and then an equal amount to the left on the next hop. When the skis come down, let them land fairly flat and let them turn by themselves for just a fraction of a second before the next hop. You will soon have a respectable wedeln run under way. Good wedeln needs perfect rhythm.

Hopping to Control

by Philip Miller, Certified, NRMSIA

One of the places where the style of the wedeln skier often breaks down is on steep and narrow terrain. He has learned wedeln in ideal conditions, or nearly so, but finds that he cannot use it to go down the fall line when things get tough.

The answer is an increase in lift.

The best way to work up more controlled wedeln turns is to go back to ideal conditions and do the following exercises, then go up again to the expert terrain and do the exercise there.

The skier should pick a moderately steep hill, one that has a nice outrun so he can break off at any time and run the hill out. Start the exercise not too far above the outrun at first.

Take your starting position by going into a steep traverse and putting the pole into the snow as in the start of a normal wedeln turn. Now, instead of letting the skis stay on the snow in the turn and using minimum lift to execute the turn, jump the skis through the entire turn (see illustration). Then jump them back again to make the next turn. The less the skis are on the snow the better.

The object of the exercise is to make the maximum number of turns in the shortest distance. Now do the same on the steep terrain, but with added comma so you are leaning farther away from the hill. You will find that you now can handle this expert terrain.

VIII. *Techniques for Racing*

The recreational skier may not be aware of it, but his basic information was developed out of ski racing. This was not always true. The Arlberg, first of the widespread American techniques, was based on a reliable Army turn, not a racing turn. But since the early 1950's, advances in the sport can be traced to the ranks of the racers and the studies of men like Kruckenhauser, Brandenberger and Testa in Europe. Analysis of racing technique by means of the camera may be expected to bring more changes in recreational technique in future years. The same is true of cross-country: an article on touring, based on the new cross-country racing technique, is included for the sake of that small but growing number of skiers who are taking up this rewarding facet of the sport.

The pointers and articles in this section are aimed at making better racers out of good ones, and toward helping place the U.S. among the top three Alpine nations as a constant threat and, in the not-too-distant future, an occasional take-all winner.

The Hottest Turn of All

by Tom Corcoran

Undoubtedly the most common piece of gratuitous advice given a slalom runner is to "Get high." If a run is slow the invariable response has always been, "you weren't high enough." Over the years the mere repetition of this adage has created an aura of truth around it, despite evidence to the contrary.

Most racers have had runs at one time or another in slalom or giant slalom that they considered near ideal—until their time was announced. If you fall in a race or make an obvious blunder you can understand a poor time, but it gets to your psyche when you can't find fault with a run (you were high in every gate!), but your result is inexplicably slow.

Or the converse can happen. You lose your line in the first gate, find yourself low in every gate, sometimes in the loose snow below the track, and you cross the finish line disgusted with yourself. To your not inconsiderable surprise you find that you have fired a fast one. In thinking back, all you can recall is a general feeling of sloppiness and sort of a desperate quality to the run. You were continually worried about making the next gate because you were so low. Somehow you made all the gates. Somehow you were fast. Why?

Both of these examples are familiar and both examples should lead a racer to look critically at the "get high" adage. I went through this sort of soul-searching just before the Olympics in 1960 and reached some conclusions which I credit for my fourth place in the Olympic giant slalom. I didn't invent anything, and a number of other racers seem to have reached the same conclusions independently at about the same time. Ironically, giant slalom was my worst event at the beginning of the 1960 season. I felt there was something about it that I didn't quite understand. After the team was selected in late December, we went to Europe for a month of warm-up races, starting with the Hahnenkamm in Kitzbühel, then into Switzerland for three more at Lenzerheide, St. Moritz and Davos. In Kitzbühel I began to question for the first time whether the high line was necessarily best. Before we reached Switzerland, I had decided that I didn't have much to lose in trying a different tack. I reversed the adage; I wouldn't be any higher in a gate than I had to be to make the next one. I wouldn't worry about sloppiness, and I would aim straight for the inside pole of each succeeding gate. The key question in this approach was: when and how would I make the turn?

My thinking went back to the hours of practice spent by Guttorm Berge, Ernie McCulloch, Bill Tibbetts, myself and others in the early 50's. Berge had developed a kind of step turn for back-and-forth open gates on steep pitches and the rest of us worked on it also. We used it for recovery purposes, when, by accident, we were too low to do anything else. I am sure many racers before us also used a step turn in one way or another.

It seemed to me, in 1960, that this same turn could be used not just for recovery but as a general rule. And it occurred to me that it would probably be more effective in gates on a flat than on steep places.

I tried out the theories in giant slaloms at Lenzerheide in the Phillips Rennen and at Davos in the Gold Cup. I came second at Lenzerheide and won at Davos against a field containing some racers slated for first seeding in the Olympics. At Squaw Valley I ran late in second seeding and came fourth. If I had run earlier I think I would have earned a medal. Staub, who won, and a number of others, including some Americans, had reached the same conclusions I had. Recalling the supremacy of Toni Sailer in the middle 50's I am certain that he was the first racer to use the step turn as it is being used today, and this fact accounted for his overwhelming margins of victory in giant slalom.

The step turn now is generally recognized as being the fastest technique for giant slalom and slalom. All of our Olympic men's teams use it, as do the top racers in other countries.

Here, in capsule form, is an outline of the turn.

Description: As you approach the inside pole of a gate with all your weight on the lower ski, pick up the tip of your unweighted upper ski and place it on a higher traverse, thus splitting the tips. Weight the uphill ski fully with a sharp up motion, usually with both hands swinging up in front at the same time. Continue to swing your weight up onto the uphill ski until it becomes momentarily unweighted. As the uphill ski is unweighted, turn it into the fall line. Simultaneously place the unweighted lower ski beside it and drop into a moderate reverse as you pass the inside pole. Come to a square position on your skis as you come out of the fall line. Go straight toward the inside pole of the next gate and step up five to twenty-five feet before you reach the pole in the same way described above. The distance required is a judgment factor and varies with your speed and the sharpness of the turn.

THE STEP TURN ILLUSTRATED

(Top to bottom.) (1) Step is made. Note split tips. Weight is shifted to uphill ski. (2) Uphill hand (left) comes up sharply, partially unweighting uphill ski. Body twists downhill to turn uphill ski into fall line. Lower ski is picked up to come in close to left ski. (3) Upper ski has been turned downhill. Body is relatively erect from up-unweighting. Lower ski is placed next to upper ski. (4) Step turn is completed as racer passes inside pole in conventional position of moderate reverse.

Why is the turn faster? A straight line between two gates is the fastest line. When you step up into a higher traverse just before you reach the gate you have changed your direction with little loss of momentum and little, if any, skid. When you unweight your uphill ski and turn it into the fall line, you have dropped into the same track you would have pursued if you had followed a high line, but you have reached that point sooner.

Furthermore, the distribution of speed throughout the turn is different. When you follow a high line, you are relatively slow across the traverse to the point above the next gate, where you start your turn. Then, as you turn down toward the gate, you accelerate, with the result that you might have to make a second turn as you pass the gate in order to be high for the next gate. The higher you are, the slower your traverse will be, and the greater the acceleration into the gate, which is the place where you least need it because it normally results in forcing you to make a second turn in the same gate. To eliminate the second turn, you might traverse farther across the hill before turning down toward the gate, but this just increases the distance you have to cover and is even slower.

With a step turn, the traverse is obviously faster because it is closer to the fall line. If you feel you are going too fast to hold the turn, you can step up earlier and make your turn with a longer radius, which makes it easier to control your speed as you pass the flag. Or, if you feel you can hold your speed in the turn, you can wait until the last moment before stepping up and turning, thus carrying almost all your traverse speed into the turn.

Basically, you want to build up maximum speed in a hurry in the traverse phase. In the turn itself, speed is less important than accuracy. If

you turn in the right place (close to the pole) and head straight for the next gate, you will not have to worry much about acceleration; it will take care of itself.

How do you learn it? Every turn you make in every "fun" run down every hill has to be a step turn. At first it will be awkward because both legs have to be taught to operate independently, but soon you will find you can do it to one extent or another on any kind of hill in any snow condition. It has to become automatic so that you do it instinctively. Then you are ready for gates. Try it first with single poles, set quite loosely on a flat hill. Then tighten the gates up, put them on steep hills and mix them up with combinations. In combinations a step turn is only applicable for the first entry turn. With the splitting of your skis near slalom gates you might worry about hooking tips. With reasonable care and practice you won't hook any more than you usually do, and you might hook less.

You will find: (1) that a step up on a steep hill is not easy and only a small step is possible; (2) that the more you are out of the fall line the harder it is to take a big step and still finish it; (3) it is more effective on flat terrain.

There is a tendency to cut off your turn too early and step up too soon. Make sure that the lower ski is tracking for the next inside pole after every turn. Do not get into extreme body positions; you can only step from a square position.

The step turn does take judgment, and it is not for a novice. For the advanced recreational skier, it's handy on a mogulled slope because you can step up and around the moguls. It takes much more strength to use than conventional feet-together skiing, and is more fatiguing, but the result is worth the effort.

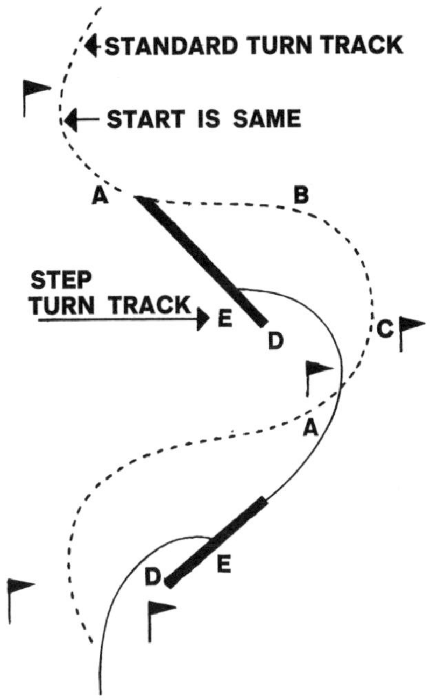

ADVANTAGE OF A STEP TURN TO THE STANDARD APPROACH

Standard approach: racer is slowest in traverse phase of turns (A to B) because he is on a high traverse, far out of fall line. From points B to C, racer turns well above inside pole of gate. From C to inside pole, racer accelerates. This creates a problem. If acceleration is too great, racer will have to turn again at point A to remain in high line to next gate. In effect, this requires two turns, with two skids in one gate, a time consuming maneuver. Racer is slowest during traverse which is the easiest part and should be utilized fully. Racer is fastest as he approaches inside pole, where greatest control and least speed is needed. Step turn approach: traverse phase of turn (A to D) is run at maximum speed because racer is taking straightest line possible between inside poles of gates. At point E, racer steps up on uphill ski, thus changing direction slightly without skid or appreciable loss of momentum. Uphill ski is immediately turned downhill and racer passes inside pole of gate in same position as if he had followed high line, but sooner. The actual turn and passing of inside pole are more easily controlled and carved in conventional manner.

SKI POINTERS FOR THE RACER

by Willy Schaeffler, Director, Arapahoe Basin Ski School, Colorado

Start of Turn in Steep Slalom

In a steep slalom course, or on very steep terrain, it is easier to start a turn with two poles than with one. The two poles will not only help you unweight, but will also give you a pivot point and a double push instrument to get under way.

The turn should be executed at the end of the up movement. Heels are barely lifted and edge change takes place in the air. Ski tips should never lose the feel with the snow.

The same maneuver can, of course, be done with one pole, but then it requires much more unweighting.

Skating Steps

In making comparative tests, it has been found that skating steps are used by almost eighty per cent of all racers of all calibers, but that very few get any advantage out of their skating attempt. The main reason is that they are not executing the skating step as it should be executed. It should be used just as it is by the speed skater—to throw and shift the weight of the body in a general forward direction, from one leg to the other, by using the inside edge for control and as a base for starting a powerful forward move. The poles play a very important part, too.

The skating step must be a completely coordinated movement of precision timing of body shift and leg action. Balance and timing will accelerate the racer very definitely, especially at lower speeds. The skating step can be used in flat starts and finishes and in slower sections of a slalom or giant slalom course. It requires a great deal of practice if it is to be useful. Tests made with different members of my ski team showed differences of up to three seconds in a skating distance of forty yards.

Step Turn

This is a quick and rythmical turn that every slalom racer should know, and it is a very simple one to carry out. It is a form of stem turn, and the preparation for it is basically the same as the stem christie. The turn is initiated with less up-unweighting than you would normally use for a parallel turn, but with more thorough weight shift from one leg to the other.

To make a racing step turn, brush the unweighted, uphill ski lightly over the snow into a stemmed position, always maintaining contact between the snow and the inside edge of the ski so that you will not lose the feel of the snow. Now, put your weight firmly onto the uphill ski and start the turn at the very same moment.

You will find that this is a very rhythmical movement and a much quicker way of getting around than a turn that is started with an unweighting movement only.

Straddling of Poles

Straddling of slalom poles can be avoided very simply by adopting a basic rule: finish a turn before entering the gate line and keep a distance from the pole of approximately one to one and a half feet. If a racer is any closer to the pole than this, he must dodge it, which can cause all kinds of trouble.

This method of avoiding slalom poles puts the racer into a good starting position for his next maneuver and allows him to make steadier, surer and safer slalom runs.

Start Position

A good start has often won a very important race. Today, more than ever before in modern racing, one can observe sloppy starts among the top racers. *Since in most races the first twenty or thirty feet after the starting gate is rather flat and slow, it is most important to reach high speed right from the starting gate.* This can be done by taking the right body position. Both poles are planted in front of the starting gate. One ski boot tip is up to the start line, the other not more than one foot behind, and feet are approximately one foot apart. Skis point exactly in the direction you have to go. Ankles, knees and hips are bent in low flexed position. Weight is on balls of feet, ready to spring forward using merely the power of the legs. The push with the poles is blended in with the leg work. One or two more powerful pole pushes will help to accelerate faster and bring you quickly to your racing speed.

IX. *Special Conditions and Situations*

Skiers who have conquered the motions of skiing through wedeln soon learn that the terrain and the quality of the snow now become the challenge rather than disciplining the body to learning new movements. And judgment plays a strong role: how much heel thrust, pole work, modification of angulation and so on. The following articles and pointers are aimed at sharpening the skier's wits and adding a trick or two to his repertory.

Meeting Four Ski Challenges

by Junior Bounous

In today's world, skis are used to experience the thrill of doing something without being motorized. Gravity gives us speed, and speed makes the body feel light in weight. This lets the skier dance down the slope with freedom of movement that would be impossible standing still. So freedom becomes part of skiing, not only in movement but also in thought. Daily routines are forgotten in the dash down the mountain, replaced by a concentration on the challenge of each turn on new terrain. The terrain is ever-changing. And, happily, the snow rarely stays the same. Most often it changes by the hour. New trails, challenges of changing snow and challenges of changing terrain hold the interest of the best of skiers. The following demonstrations show how to meet and enjoy four challenges of terrain and snow.

CHALLENGE ONE: DROP-OFF

The first turn (below) meets the challenge of more difficult terrain—a drop-off. This fast turn is begun with a quick down motion. The down movement is necessary to absorb the effect of the bump so the skis stay in contact with the snow, under control. The bump is approached with a high body position, and the body is dropped to the lowest position on top of the bump. There is then a gradual straightening of legs to return to a normal position. Step by step:

1. Normal position on approach to bumpy terrain.
2. As skis cross hollow in approach to next bump, there is a straightening of legs to better position the skier for absorbing the sharpness in the approaching bump.
3. At the peak of the bump the legs have bent to the lowest point to absorb shock of bump. Turning power is applied to change the skis' direction.
4. Edges have now changed, and skis are pointing into a new direction.
5. Skis are following around turn, and legs are straightened to return to a normal position.

CHALLENGE TWO: HEADWALL

The second challenge is to control speed on the steep terrain of a sheer headwall. The secret here is to swing the tails of the skis quickly through the fall line to a wide-angle position where the edges are set. The quick fanning motion of the skis and the hard edge-set means the skis will not gain speed. Both poles are used to aid the unweighting. This helps bring the weight forward at unweighting so the tails of the skis stay in the air for a longer period of time. The tails of the skis travel forty-five to fifty degrees in the air. Then they land and continue to slide around to a wide angle with the fall line before they are set. The total amount of displacement is determined by the amount of braking you want. The slower you want to go, the wider the angle from the fall line before each edge set. Step by step:

1. Arms are extended forward in position for planting both poles.

2. Both poles are planted as ski edges are set ready for the unweighting. Knees and ankles are well bent into a position from which to spring up.

3. The poles are carrying some of the weight as the legs have straightened to spring from the snow. The skis are pulled up with bent knees.

4. The skis are back on the snow. The outside pole comes free of the snow before the inside one. The body moves in a down motion.

5. Fanning motion is complete. The arms and poles are again started forward, edge-setting starts.

CHALLENGE THREE: FATIGUE

The next challenge is the challenge of fatigue. It is met by the parallel turn shown above—the idealized form furnished by the American Technique. This is the parallel turn performed under easy conditions of terrain, snow and speed. In these ideal conditions, the American system turn is almost effortless. A minimum of energy is used and the body is relaxed. It is a simple turn that can be used mile after mile without tiring. It minimizes fatigue on long, rolling trails. Step by step:

1. A slight down to set edges before the up.

2. Up motion from ankles and knees to unweight and transfer weight to outside ski.

3. The turning of the skis by counter motion. Skis have changed direction, but shoulders have remained in nearly the same position as previous figure.

4. Down motion in order to complete the counter motion and to get body into angle position to control edging.

5. The body follows the skis in comfortable, relaxed position, exerting a minimum of effort.

CHALLENGE FOUR: SOGGY SPRING SNOW

The last turn meets the challenge of sun- and water-soaked spring snow on a steep hill. To meet this challenge, use a two-pole, slow-speed christie. This turn, like all the other turns in this article, is within the systems of the American Technique. The particular modifications of this turn are: First, more emphasis on the up-unweighting. Second, a lower, stable body position to offset the resistance of the heavy snow. Third, the unweighting is started from a lower body position and is followed by an upward pull of the feet so skis are clear of the snow longer. Both poles are used, not only for balance but also to support the upward movement of the feet in the unweighting phase.

Upon landing, the body crouches lower to prevent your being thrown off balance because of heavy snow resistance. The amount of angulation needed for edging is small because the snow is soft and speed is low. Step by step:

1. Deep position affected by bending ankles and knees. The poles are placed well forward for correct timing to aid in the unweighting.

2. The upper body is pushed straight upward. The legs lift the skis clear of the snow. Generally, the skis are turned no farther than the fall line before coming back into the snow. A common mistake is to try to turn too far.

3. Poles are removed from the snow. The turn is cut off quickly and then repeated.

Ski the Bowls with Stein

by Stein Eriksen

The bowl is basically a trail where the sides rise high enough to give a skier plenty of room for a wide sweeping turn on one side followed by a high sweeping turn on the other. Not only is bowl skiing great fun but you can learn a lot from it. If you fall in a bowl turn, you will either fall up the hill or across the hill so a fall is not serious. You can afford to experiment, to push yourself. You can learn to get maximum enjoyment out of the turns by reaching the maximum speed in each turn.

Because I have learned how to ski them, I enjoy the bowls more, perhaps, than anything else. A bowl turn gives me that tremendous feel

of speed and graceful soaring. I use the wall of a bowl to challenge gravity and win that challenge.

I first developed my liking for bowls in the winter of 1953 at Sun Valley. I remember the Easter Bowl, Christmas Bowl and all the Sun Valley bowls stretching down from that high ridge in the middle of the Idaho mountains. I loved to make long sweeping turns from side to side. That winter of 1953, Christian Pravda was there and so was Jack Reddish. We raced against each other on weekends, but during the week, when we skied for fun, we skied the bowls. I can still remember the wonderful feeling I got when I first learned to go up high on each wall.

Bowl skiing has contributed a lot to my style, first as a racer and then as a ski school head. Most good racers today exhibit great similarity to the kind of skiing that you learn when you practice bowl turns. So if you have never felt the sensation of a real high-speed reverse-shoulder turn, why not try the bowls?

In bowl skiing, I keep rediscovering how important it is to get your body weight to the inside of a high-speed turn, at the same time keeping your legs at a low angle to the snow so that you can jam the edges in and fight centrifugal force. The faster the turn, the closer the legs should get to the snow. The lower-body lean toward the inside will give you a real hard-driving, perfectly controlled turn at high speed. The upper body, of course, somewhat makes up for the inward lean of the lower body by bending toward the outside of the turn.

The lower-body lean enables you to carve the turn in a true arc with no slipping. This wide, carving turn is something that you can transfer to your non-bowl skiing.

Here, step by step, is how I do the bowl turn.

I start on the floor of the bowl between the two walls. I am in a fast traverse. Then comes the important part. I start my turn almost as soon as I start to climb the wall of the bowl. The first move in starting the turn is a slight check that puts the weight on the inside ski. From there I lift off slightly from both skis and as I come down I put my weight on the outside ski. But I do this very carefully. I want the turn to stretch out.

I try to get in the reverse position now, to start powering the turn around. I pull the outside hip and shoulder back and back as the turn gets going. Not only does reversing the shoulder and hip help power the turn but it lets me slant the legs close to the snow, and lets me lean the upper body out to counterbalance.

The weight is on my outside ski from the time I land until the very end of the turn. Looking at these pictures it may appear that I can't possibly have the weight on the outside ski in that position, but I do. The more speed I have, the more I lean inward and the less likely it seems that I have my weight on the outside ski. But the extra centrifugal force generated by the high-speed turn lets me keep the weight firmly on that outside ski.

As the turn progresses, my body slowly comes around to "lead" the turn. Finally, toward the end I start squaring my position and let my legs come up away from the snow so that I am standing straighter. Warning: don't square off and stand up too early. I maintain that in bowl skiing the hip particularly should not come around to a square position until you are in the gully again.

Now for the over-all rule: "let yourself go." In bowl skiing there should never be a dull moment. You have to get into it with a little abandon in order to get the proper spirit. The foundation of it all is conscientious practice, together with a flair for having fun while you do practice.

By the end of a season of bowl turns, you should be the possessor of a hard-driving racing turn that you can use anywhere on the hill.

Stay with the bowls and your new high-speed turn will stay with you.

SKI POINTERS ON SPECIAL CONDITIONS AND SITUATIONS

Two Poles for Mashed Potatoes

by Miner Patton, Certified, PNSIA

The soft, wet, heavy snow that is known as "mashed potatoes" can be a terrific problem for the parallel skier. He finds that his lift is not enough to get him around and that trying to lift more soon makes him tired.

The clue to working your way down a mashed potato slope is to get the skis around in the air fast so that they come down forcefully in an arc that continues as they land.

If you find that your normal lift and pole work does not do the job, then the two pole turn is the answer.

Try bringing both poles forward for each turn, fairly far apart, and set them both in the snow with a down motion of the knees. Now spring up and at the same time lift the tails deliberately high, displace them a rather short distance in the direction of the turn and let them drop into the snow again (see illustration).

The stability afforded by two poles, the lift that can be applied to the skis and the turning power that can be generated after the tails have been displaced only a few inches will make it possible to continue skiing through the thickest slop on the slope.

Do Not Hesitate

by Georgia Hotton, Certified, RMSIA; Member, PSIA

Sticky, slushy snow may be encountered at any time of year, but it is common in spring. The worst that can happen is that slushy snow will ice up on your skis. This means you will have to stop and scrape. To avoid icing up, when you come to an area of slushy snow keep moving. Remember to *have your weight forward and use your poles to get you across if necessary. Once you hit the other side, keep on going for a while.* If you stop or hesitate on the far side of a slushy spot, the colder, drier snow may freeze the slush to your skis. The skier who crosses a slushy spot and stops to wait for his friends to catch up may be iced to a stop when they are going past him.

Powder Technique

by Leo Olson, Certified, PNSIA, Member, PSIA

In a fresh fall of powder snow, a strong rotation or reverse of the upper or lower body in an attempt to turn the skis may bring disaster. Strong moves will throw the weight on one ski or the other, but in powder it is necessary to keep the weight on both skis nearly equal. Gentle horizontal movements will serve to govern change of direction. Therefore, if you have started a turn in powder and then you feel it needs an extra touch to bring you around, don't rotate your shoulders or thrust your heels: just *bring the hand on the outside of the turn forward another six or eight inches, allowing the shoulder to follow naturally* (*see arrow in illustration*). It will not disturb the even weighting of the skis and may be all you need to complete the turn easily and naturally.

Stepping Through Powder

by Otto Ost, Certified, PNSIA

Powder snow is a cause for rejoicing among the skiers who are used to it: they have developed their techniques for handling powder and find it easy skiing. But the stem skier who hasn't had a chance to work out a feel for powder is often at a loss.

There is a very easy and direct way of skiing powder that can be picked up in a few minutes by a stem skier. It involves a sort of step stem that will move you through the snow in the fall line—getting out of the fall line is the major fault of the new powder skier.

Take a nice powder slope with a safe runout and practice the step stem a few times: just start down the fall line and fan one ski out in a slight stem. Put your weight on the stemmed ski immediately, just as if you were stepping on it. Now step back onto the other ski, then back to the first, using a slight stem each time (see illustration).

You will turn each time you step, and this will be enough, in powder, to keep you under control. You must ski pretty much in the fall line in powder, to begin with, and probably you will have to ski faster than you are used to skiing in packed snow. Keep in the fall line, keep speed and keep stepping.

Pop Over the Patch

by Earl M. Leichter, Certified, CSIA

Many skiers are clumsy on ice patches. They skid, fall and struggle. Provided that the hill is not all ice and that the patches are reasonably small, six to ten feet across, there is a fine way to handle them.

Prior to entering the ice patch, lower the upper body by pressing the knees forward and sitting at the hips. The moment the skis touch ice, come up suddenly, just as in a normal unweighting maneuver. This unweights your skis over the ice. (Don't jump them over the patch: getting your weight off is enough.) Now the skis will run straight over, and, when you come down, you can set your edges in a controlled heel thrust to cut down on the speed you have picked up.

If you don't have to cut speed, then advance your uphill ski for a steadier landing as you come down and continue on.

Taking the weight off the skis lets them cross the ice without wavering, chattering or throwing you off your form: it's the easy way over an ice patch.

Sink and Set 'Em

by Starr Brinckerhoff, Certified, USEASA; Member, PSIA

Do you find yourself unable to control your speed on steep bumpy slopes? If so, your difficulty might come from failing to make that "set" or down motion at the end of one turn, which simultaneously becomes the preparatory position for the next. The down motion (arrow) serves to sink the edges of the skis well into the snow. Sink down vigorously into an exaggerated comma position so that your weight bears heavily on both skis, particularly the outside ski of the turn. In so doing, you will find that you exert great braking power on your speed and gain precision in the turn. Your edge set becomes more effective. That, coupled with the up motion that puts you into the next turn, will enable you to shorten the radius of your turns. In effect, your accentuated set or drop leads to a longer up motion and this makes it easier to swing the skis into the next turn. The turns become easier when you move from comma to comma with a long, sailing up motion between each precisely controlled set.

On Skiing Moguls

by Bob Bourdon, Certified, USEASA

If you can do a fair parallel turn, here is a way to ski moguls with more fun and half the effort. First, make a forward sideslip toward the top of a mogul. As you approach the top of the mogul, *use heel thrust to place the skis at a right angle to your line of descent.* Now, edge the skis to check your speed, using a normal knee and pole action. Next, release the edges and turn the skis to the new direction, pivoting on the crown of the mogul. Continue in this manner. In this way you will stay close to the fall line and ski at just the speed you like. You will not bounce erratically from one mogul to the next, tired and half out of control. Remember to keep the skis flat and slipping except at the moment you check your speed on the "up side" of the mogul. Flat skis turn effortlessly on the top of a mogul, so you need only the slightest up and down motion to unweight your skis for the turn.

River Running

by Frank Lamphier, Certified, USEASA; Member, PSIA

On steep bumpy terrain there is a more or less precise method of keeping it simple: *the good skier who wants the most effortless way to get down should think of what he is doing as "two traverse positions plus a sideslip."*

The traverses are steep ones—either to the skier's left or to the right.

The intermediate position is the sideslip (actually a sideslip across the fall line) shown below, opposite page.

But primarily, the technique calls for checking your speed against the uphill side of the mogul, as shown in top illustration, and sliding through the groove between it and the next mogul as below, opposite page.

The hips and shoulders point down the fall line so that, in effect, you are wiggling your way down a river of moguls, always facing "downstream." The technique has been called "river running."

The essence of it is turning above and between the moguls rather than, as in slower intermediate skiing, turning over the tops of the moguls.

The Light Touch

by H. F. Haemisegger, Certified, FWSIA; Member, PSIA

In rough spring snow, skiing rigidly or tightly can lead to major problems—edge catching, stiff, jerky turns or falls. A relaxed run can make all elements of skiing easier, more enjoyable and safer. However, even the advanced skier finds himself tightening up at times, especially on his first run of the day. An easy way to help loosen up is to hold your ski poles lightly. Not, of course, so lightly that they dangle uselessly behind you. If you feel tense, just *stretch your hand, flex the fingers for a minute and assume a new hand grip on the pole.* Make sure the pole is more or less resting on your fingertips, not locked in a grip of iron. Whenever you feel tense, start with your fingers to relax your whole body.

Spring Through Slush

by John Kronsnoble, Certified, CUSSA; Member, PSIA

Everyone knows that good spring skiing is one of the greatest thrills of the sport. Occasionally, however, you will find that while the sun's effect on the top of the mountain is perfect, it has been devastating farther down. As you descend to lower altitudes and increasing temperatures, a sea of slush greets you. The thing to remember when you find yourself in this situation is to handle it like deep powder. In other words, sit back just enough to offset the increased friction of the slush and its suction on the bottoms and sides of your skis. Second, *exaggerate the down-up-down of your turns* (*see illustration*). Third, in a turn keep the edging of your skis equal and at a minimum. Then your turns will be smooth, even in mashed potato snow.

Foil Spring Suction

by Edward S. Pelkey, Certified, RMSIA; Member, PSIA

In skiing soft, sticky spring snow, skiers sometimes find themselves walking a considerable distance after a run to the lift lines because their skis simply won't move through the snow at the runout. This is particularly true when there is a fairly long, flat schuss at the end. The reason is that suction caused by the wet snow slows skis down. This can be avoided and good speed maintained longer if the skier will continually lift one ski and then the other (see illustration). This breaks the suction effect and lets the skis maintain a higher speed through the runout.

X. *Conditioning*

The sure-fire, two-second conditioning exercise that will permit a secretary to shed her high heels and the overwrought executive his business suit and step fully primed into her and his skis and take off down the slope without a twinge of a muscle is not yet invented. However, care in selecting a few exercises will help. The person involved is the only one who knows the extent to which he wants to stretch himself in his skiing, and he should pick his exercises accordingly. In general, it is probably better to do a very few exercises regularly than to do a lot with great fury at longer intervals. Any exercise which gives the skier a more effective ski position or understanding of how to use his musculature more effectively is a valuable one, no matter how mild. And, in skiing, posture and positioning mean as much or more as brute strength, any day.

Stand Right, Ski Right

by Monica Saxon

As a New York ballerina with a lively business in corrective therapy as a sideline, I have worked with skiers, football players, boxers and Saturday sportsmen for a number of years, straightening out physical kinks for them. I have found in this work that in each sport, as in daily living, there is a proper way to stand and there are proper ways to move. In skiing, I have found that the average person is strong enough to ski, provided he or she skis in a relaxed, muscle-saving manner. Second, I have found that "skiing is moving." You may look strong standing still, but you have to be able to move freely. These exercises will give you: (1) the basic stance, (2) basic moves for the sport.

The basic stance is a position that I call "standing on your skeleton," a position that is in remarkable agreement with the concepts of the American system as formed by the PSIA instructors. The idea of this basic position is that it balances the body so that the weight is carried into the floor by the bone structure. The first exercise is to get a full-length mirror and try to assume the basic stance yourself. Here's how: first, draw a deep breath to expand the chest as far as it will go. Now, keep the chest expanded, as in the illustration at the far left. Breathe without moving the chest, but simply by moving the muscles of the diaphragm area inward and outward. Move the area out to inhale and draw it in to exhale. The chest stays up, way up. This expansion of the chest lines up the vertebrae of the backbone one atop the other in the best alignment to carry the weight of the upper body. The arms are held well back. The hips are tucked under the chest and thrust forward until they seem to be under and *in front* of the chest. The chin is in toward the neck as far as it can go. Now, let the weight of the entire body be carried down the outside of both legs into the outside rim and heel of the foot (not the arch) and from there into the floor. This stance puts the weight of the head on top of the spine, the weight of the chest is carried around to the middle spine, the weight from the spine is easily transmitted to the girdle of bones at the hip, from the hip down the legs to the outside of the feet and into the floor. This spares the muscles. At first, some of the muscles will ache a bit when the body is fully stretched into position. This is because you have been standing in the wrong, bent-forward position (see illustration), which throws the weight on the back muscle. Practice breathing in the basic stance for two or three minutes, then ten minutes. Skiers who faithfully practice the basic position will have ski-ready muscles.

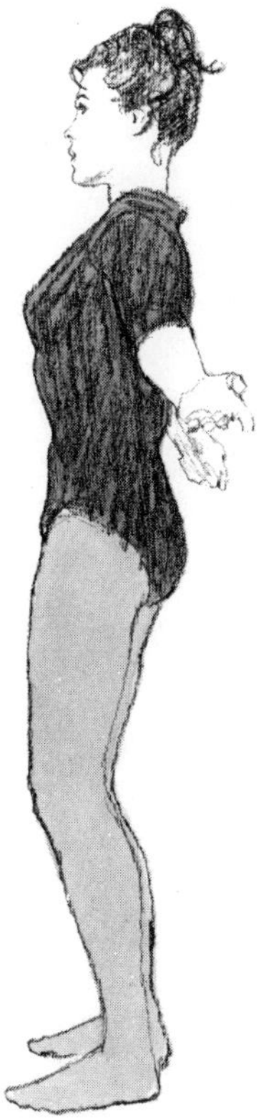

Slow motion arm stretch. This is done from the basic position. The purpose is to stretch the back muscles upward and downward so they can finally relax. The exercise gets the skier automatically into the proper basic position. The exercise is done very slowly. First (below), the arms move in small circles which constantly increase in size until the arms are making large circles. The hands come to rest at the bottom of the last large circle. From there, the arms are raised slowly (bottom, opposite page) until they come to an overhead position. The arms then drop slowly until the basic position is reached. Repeat the whole cycle once and then go back to the breathing exercise for a few minutes. This should bring the backbone into line and gently stretch the back muscles. The result is a body well relaxed.

The leg flop is a before-and-after ski exercise. It is designed to persuade the legs to relax if they feel stiff in the morning or if they are tired and tight after a hard day's skiing. Essentially, you lift one leg in a straight position (nearest leg in the illustration), then the leg is allowed to fall right to the floor in a straight position. (You may think this will hurt, but it won't.) While the near leg is dropping, the other leg is picked up in a bent position (see far leg) preparatory to straightening and lifting. The legs are alternately lifted and dropped to the floor with a resounding thump, muscles relaxed. This will loosen the stiff inner muscles of the leg, increase the circulation of the blood in the legs and ready them for skiing the next day. During the exercise, the skier's chest should remain expanded and breathing should be done by raising and lowering the diaphragm.

The thigh stretcher is a muscle-lengthener for the muscles of the buttock and thigh. These muscles must be easily stretchable in order that the skier can go into a crouch quickly and smoothly. The exercise starts in the basic position and the skier bends forward (left below). As the bend continues, the skier should check the mirror to see that the legs remain vertical. The bend should start right at the hip joint and not at the waist. Fully bent, the skier (right below) should still have legs vertical and backbone fairly straight.

Balanced knee bend is not primarily a strengthening exercise but a "movement" exercise. The goal is to stay in a balanced skeleton stance while bending the knees. This is the position that the skier should use on the hill rather than the forward-leaning crouch. This exercise particularly requires a mirror. The exercise begins with the skier dropping directly down onto the heels, keeping the back straight and chest expanded. In the full crouch, the back is still erect.

Jumping jack is another movement exercise designed to show the skier the right way to perform the "lift" of parallel skiing. The exercise starts in the basic position. The skier drops halfway toward the floor and then jumps straight up in a full stretch that brings the feet up off the floor. Perform the exercise in place, being sure to land solidly each time. Next, instead of jumping straight up, jump backward a foot or two. Try to increase this to a yard or more. This latter variation is a balance-improver. Skiers often lose balance simply because they tense whenever their skiing causes them to start tipping backward. The backward-jump exercise lessens the skier's tendency to tense and makes recovery much easier.

5BX Plan for Skiers

by Dr. William Orban, Originator of the Royal Canadian Air Force Exercises

Maximum enjoyment and health may be derived from skiing at any age—but only if you have an adequate level of physical condition. To help skiers of any age achieve proper conditioning, I have designed a program of four basic exercises in three series—beginner, intermediate and advanced. In addition, there is a bonus exercise. The five exercises have been selected for their contribution to the conditioning of the muscles and joints which play an important role in skiing.

The first exercise is a mobilizing exercise which is designed to produce a greater range of movement, of a rotational nature, in the ankles, knees and spinal column. Exercise two will develop the abdominal muscles which are used in the trunk and hip rotation so essential for certain maneuvers in skiing. It will also provide an additional opportunity to improve the mobility of the spinal column. Exercise three is primarily for the development of lower and upper back muscles on which there is an additional demand in the skiing posture. Exercise three, particularly in the advanced series, will also improve the strength of the upper arm muscles needed for pole action. Exercise four is the key exercise for strengthening the lower muscles of the limbs used in skiing as well as for strengthening the knee and ankle joints which are so prone to injury. The exercise also provides practice in dynamic balance if hands are kept on hips and an attempt is made to exercise by jumping on designated marks on the floor. Exercise five lays particular emphasis on strengthening the lower leg.

My exercises, when regularly performed, are designed to improve physical condition in a minimum length of time without any soreness or stiffness. The exercises may be performed by men or women at any age, with maximum benefits, so long as the directions for performing them are carefully and accurately followed. If you have any previous medical history which makes you feel uncertain about following the 5BX program, you should obtain your physician's approval before starting.

Physical conditioning will enable you to engage in skiing for more hours per day, more days per week and more years in a lifetime. It also will contribute to the prevention of injuries. Many injuries, particularly of the sprain variety, can be attributed to poor physical condition. Lack of strength in the muscles involved in skiing and lack of strength and mobility in the joints, particularly in the knees and ankles, contribute to the incidence of injuries. Furthermore, lack of organic and muscular endurance increases the onset of fatigue, frequently cited as a prime cause of injuries among weekend skiers.

Skiers should maintain a year-round program of training for maximum benefit. A minimum training period would be ten weeks prior to the first ski outing. Any program, to be beneficial and effective, must be followed regularly and frequently. Regularity implies a definite time per day and no less than five days per week. The program for skiers was designed to be followed five days a week for a minimum of ten weeks.

The principles of progression and overload have been completely utilized in the program. Progression enables the development of physical condition from a very low level to a very high level by increasing the rate at which each exercise is regularly and gradually performed. Each exercise, while remaining basically the same, increases in intensity (difficulty because of increased resistance) as you graduate from series to series.

It's important, therefore, when you undertake the exercises—regardless of your present physical condition—that you start with the first level of the beginner series in order to prevent discomfort. No matter how physically fit you may feel, you are courting trouble—muscle soreness—if you undertake a new exercise without specifically conditioning your muscles for it. So perform each exercise in the unit of time given for that exercise. This means that if five repetitions of an exercise are suggested for one minute, the five repetitions should be evenly spaced so as to take the full one minute. The temptation is always present to finish them as quickly as possible, but the object is to use all of the allotted time to do each exercise. Otherwise you will incur muscle soreness.

Time units are established for individuals twenty years old or younger. Anyone over twenty should add one second for every year to the time allotted. For example, if an individual is forty years old, he should add forty seconds to the allotted time for each exercise. Women, in addition to the extra second for every year over twenty, should add another fifteen seconds to the time allotted for each exercise. This means that if a woman is forty years old, she should add forty plus fifteen, or fifty-five seconds to each exercise time unit.

In addition to the basic exercises, you should endeavor to strengthen arm and shoulder muscles by practicing regular pushups. To improve heart and lungs as well, I would heartily recommend a program of running, starting with a quarter mile (one large city block) and working up to the mile distance. Hiking in hill country also benefits both legs and wind.

For best results with the 5BX program, follow directions carefully. Perform the exercises accurately, remembering never to give in to the temptation to skip parts of the schedule or to accelerate repetitions.

Beginner Series. Exercise one: five repetitions per minute for the first five days, then add three repetitions per day for five more days. Exercise two: five repetitions per minute for first five days, add three per day for next five days. Exercise three: five repetitions per minute for the first five days, then add three per day for the next five days. Exercise four: twenty-five repetitions per two minutes, then add five per day for next five days.

Intermediate Series. Exercise one: ten repetitions per minute for five days, add two per day for ten days. Exercise two: ten repetitions per minute for first five days, add two per day for two weeks. Exercise three: ten repetitions per minute for first five days, then add two per day for ten days. Exercise four: thirty repetitions per two minutes for first five days, add seven per day for ten days.

Advanced Series. Exercise one: ten repetitions per minute for first five days, add one per day for thirty days. Exercise two: ten repetitions per minute for first five days, then add one per day for thirty days. Exercise three: ten repetitions per minute for first five days, then add one per day for thirty days. Exercise four: thirty per two minutes for five days, then add five per day for thirty days.

Exercise one: Starting position is with feet parallel and flat on floor about shoulder width apart, hands clasped behind head, elbows back. To perform the exercise, turn the upper trunk slowly toward the left, twisting as far as possible without losing balance and without moving the feet. Slowly return to starting position, then twist to the right as far as possible, allowing the hips and thighs to follow trunk without moving feet. Returning to starting position completes one repetition. This movement should be slow and performed without any jerking action.

Exercise two: Starting position is lying on back, feet straight together with arms stretched to the side, palms flat on floor. The exercise is performed by lifting the right leg across the body so that the raised foot comes directly above the left hand. The other foot and hand maintain contact with the floor during this movement. The second movement of the exercise is raising the left foot to a position over the right hand and returning to the starting position.

Exercise three: Starting position is lying flat on the back with arms by sides and hands flat on floor. The exercise is performed by lifting the buttocks just high enough to clear the floor. The complete length of the arms, shoulders, head and heels maintain contact with the floor during the entire exercise.

Exercise four: Starting position is feet astride with hands on hips. This exercise is performed by alternately jumping from one foot to the other to the outside of two imaginary parallel lines which are a leg-length apart. Cause your entire weight to shift from side to side across the parallel lines. Each time the foot touches the floor, you've completed one repetition.

Exercise one: The starting position is the same as exercise one of the beginner series except that the arms are held horizontal and at shoulder height to the trunk. Exercise is also performed in the same manner except that when the rotation is made, the head is turned to follow the arm which moved backward. The arm should be pushed as far back as possible without moving the feet. The rotation should be in a twist from the ankles and hips. One rotation with each arm completes one repetition.

Exercise two: Starting movement is the same as the beginner series. The first movement of this exercise is raising both legs simultaneously so that the left knee is almost directly over the right shoulder. The legs then are returned to the starting position. The second movement of the exercise is raising the legs so that the right knee is vertically above the left shoulder before returning to the starting position. These two movements complete one repetition of the exercise.

Exercise three: Starting position is lying on the back, arms by sides, hands flat on the floor. Now move the feet close to the buttocks by bending the knees. The buttocks should be on the floor and the feet flat before exercise is performed. The exercise is performed by raising the buttocks and forcing the hips upward as high as possible. Feet should remain flat; the head, shoulders and the entire length of the arm should maintain contact with the floor during the entire performance. Each time the hips are raised is one repetition.

Exercise four: Start with hands on hips, feet together. Exercise is performed by jumping from side to side while keeping the knees and feet together. The distance of the jumps should be between one and one-half to two foot-lengths apart. Both feet should come in full contact with the floor each time.

ADVANCE SERIES

Exercise one: Begin with the arms held across the chest with the upper arm horizontal from the shoulder. The exercise is performed by swinging the left arm backward to rotate the upper trunk, the hips, knees and ankles as far as possible without moving the feet. The first movement is completed by returning to the starting position and bending the arm. The second movement is the same only this time you're using the right arm. One repetition is completed when the initial starting position is assumed after the second movement.

Exercise two: Starting position is the same as the beginner series. Exercise is performed by raising both legs together, then lowering them to touch the floor just beyond the fingertips of the left hand before returning to starting position. The second movement of the exercise is performed by repeating first movement, but touching floor to the right. The completion of these two movements is one repetition of the exercise.

Exercise three: Starting position is the same as in exercise three of the intermediate series. The exercise is performed by raising the buttocks and the shoulders off the floor, forcing the hips and chest upward as high as possible. Force for the movement is applied at the elbows, the back of the head and the feet. Only the feet, lower arm and back of head should be in contact with the floor when hips are raised. One repetition is completed when buttocks are lowered to starting position.

Exercise four: Starting position is the same as exercise four for the intermediate series. It is performed by jumping from side to side, keeping both feet together. Distance should not be less than three foot-lengths apart. Each jump is one repetition.

Bonus exercise five: Start by placing both hands flat against a wall or some other immovable object about chest high. Then move your feet backward until heels are just making contact with the floor. Perform exercise by lifting both heels together as high as possible before lowering them to the starting position. Raising and lowering of the heels constitute one repetition.

SKI EXTRA:

Manners Maketh the Skier

by Elyse Sommer

You won't become a ski champion by observing a few simple rules of ski etiquette, but you will increase your pleasure, and everyone else's. What's more, manners among skiers contribute to safety on the hills as well as a rating with Emily Post.

Keep your place in the lift line. Ski area managers try to keep chiselers in place, but somehow there's always one around when it gets crowded.

Avoid stepping on the back of the skis of the fellow in front of you as you would avoid stepping on his feet. You may not hurt him physically, but you won't do his skis any good.

If you're alone in a busy line, double up with someone. When sharing a chair with a safety bar that lowers, make sure that you each know when the bar is coming down or you may mash some fingers. On the T-bar, don't insist on riding with someone a great deal taller or shorter than you or the ride will be uneven.

Treat a lift as you would your own equipment. Horsing around on a chair lift puts undue stress on the cables and endangers other riders. On T-bars or Pomalifts, keep your skis in the tracks and avoid the temptation to run some kind of uphill slalom. On rope tows, try to avoid jerking the rope when you get off at the top.

Move out of the way the minute you step off a lift. Sure, the view is breathtaking, but you can see it just as well a bit farther away. Mitten, goggle and binding adjustments should be performed at a distance from the debarkation point.

Ski where you belong, and ski in control. There is nothing more irritating or more dangerous than the basher who, unable to turn or stop, knocks down skiers along his way like bowling pins.

Ski defensively. If you feel a skier in front of you might make a sudden turn, warn of your own approach by calling "Track right" or "Track left" to avoid collision. This is like giving directional signals while driving, only in skiing it's done in reverse order with the one in back signaling to the one in front. If you're the front skier, take the warning and get out of the way.

Cover your sitzmarks. Leaving a hole in the snow from your fall is like preparing a trap for the next skier to catch his ski tips in.

If you stop along the way down, do so only at the side of the hill, where you will be out of the way of other skiers. And if for some reason you decide to walk instead of ski down the rest of the way, walk at the side.

Respect slalom flags set up by clubs and ski schools. If you knock down flags on a practice course, set them up again; there are others who want to run the course after you. If you are with a ski group and want to set up your own slalom flags, obtain permission from the area manager.

Put your ski gear in a rack near the slope or the lodge. Don't leave it around for others to trip on. If a pole or a ski falls down, pick it up and replace it.

If you bring box lunches be sure to check if you are allowed to eat in the general dining room or if there is a special section for picnickers. When you're finished, dispose of your refuse.

Don't spread out over more chairs than you actually need during the busy lunch hour. Other skiers want to relax, too. Sharing your table with a stranger is part of the spirit of ski camaraderie.

Look out for your own equipment. Even the smallest child should be taught to carry and put on his own ski gear.

Don't keep others waiting. A late riser has no business holding up a group of early risers. That last run before going home—the one that keeps the rest of your group waiting—is likely to be the last one you'll ever take as part of their car pool or bus.

If you're with a group occupying most of the rooms in a lodge, make the outsiders feel welcome.

If you want to have a private cocktail party, ask your ski host if it's all right with him. Some farm hosts, especially, don't like drinking on their premises, and, since it is their house, their wishes should be respected.

At night, remember that some of the best skiing is early in the morning and that many skiers don't like to burn the candle at both ends. Keep the fun as quiet as possible.

Park your car where the lot attendant at the mountain or the lodge asks you to park. Do not block access roads. They have to be plowed.

Glossary of Abbreviations of Names of Ski Associations

CSIA—Canadian Ski Instructors Alliance
CUSSA—Central United States Ski Association
CUSSIA—Central United States Ski Instructors Association
FWSA—Far West Ski Association
FWSIA—Far West Ski Instructors Association
ISA—Intermountain Ski Association
ISIA—Intermountain Ski Instructors Association
NRMSIA—Northern Rocky Mountain Ski Instructors Association
PNSA—Pacific Northwest Ski Association
PNSIA—Pacific Northwest Ski Instructors Association
PSIA—Professional Ski Instructors of America
RMSIA—Rocky Mountain Ski Instructors Association
SRMSIA—Southern Rocky Mountain Ski Instructors Association
USEASA—United States Eastern Amateur Ski Association